Garage Sale of the Mind

Garage Sale of the Mind

*Things are more like they are now
than they ever were before*

Hal Sisson
&
Dwayne Rowe

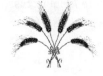

SALAL PRESS
Victoria, BC

National Library of Canada Cataloguing in Publication

Sisson, Hal C., 1921-
    Garage sale of the mind : things are more like they are now than they ever were before / Hal C. Sisson, Dwayne W. Rowe.

ISBN: 1-894012-07-0

1. Canada, Western—Social life and customs—Humor.
2. Canadian wit and humor (English). I. Rowe, Dwayne W., 1941- II. Title.

FC3206.S574 2002   971.2'002'07   C2002-904377-8
F1060.S574 2002

Cover design by Faultline Communications + Design
Cover painting by Jack McMann

Printed and bound in Canada by Transcontinental Printing

Salal Press
Box 36060
Victoria, BC V9A 7J5

To my wife Roseanne
D.W.R

To my friends of yesteryear who live on in
memory. And to Clare Thorbes, Pearl Baldwin
and my daughter Lindy Sisson for their
outstanding and enthusiastic editorial
support of my literary efforts.
H.C.S.

Contents

Introduction

We'd like to address the intelligent reader who has just picked up this book. As for the rest of you — stewed prunes!

You never know what you'll find in an attic in an old trunk or cardboard box, left by some long-deceased member of the family. The personal effects of Hal's late mother included a packet of poems copied in her handwriting. The poems date from the early twentieth century, when she taught school in places like City View, named for the faint glow of Moose Jaw lights visible in the night sky from the black hills thirty hard miles southwest of that city. Two of those poems and the stories in this book represent a garage sale of the mind for the authors. Some of Dwayne's stories are taken from pieces originally published by *Monday Magazine* in Victoria.

Before we began collaborating as writers, we were

law partners for many years. What we didn't know
about the law, we explained to each other.

It's a good thing to do once in a while—clear out
some of the old memories taking up valuable storage
space in your mind. But as we rummaged through our
respective mental attics for items to toss into this
garage sale, we realized that many of our memories
weren't politically correct by today's standards.
Nonetheless, we decided to tell it like it was, or as near
as we can remember it was.

We've also ignored the old admonitions against
discussing politics and religion in polite company.
Our garage sale contains stories about prairie politicians' shenanigans and a tale of that venerable old
institution, Sunday school, so rigorous it seemed more
inclined to encourage atheism.

In Northern Ireland during World War Two, an air
force buddy of Hal's said they wouldn't remember the
dull times, just the experiences that were meaningful,
whether good or bad. The man was right. Soon there
won't be anyone left with memories of that war, so Hal
decided to flog some of his in this curbside collection.
While in the armed forces, Hal got a letter from his
mom with news from home. He couldn't decipher a
letter in one of the words, so he asked a friend
whether it was an *i* or an *o*. "Does it really matter?" the
friend asked. Hal replied, "It sure does, 'cause if it's an
"o", my brother shot himself."

Rounding out the items on offer are reflections on
summers at the beach in Wayback, Saskatchewan, prac-
tising small-town law and the linguistic and personal
quirks of the denizens of our uniquely Canadian West.

We can still visualize the old places and experiences of our younger days, but with the attic cleared

out, even us golden-agers are free to create new memories that are just as good as the old ones. Old fogeydom isn't all that bad—think of the trouble we'd be in if wrinkles hurt! May you, dear reader, always find new roads to travel, new horizons to explore and new dreams to call your own.

Hal Sisson
Dwayne Rowe

Dog's Head Revisited

Hal Sisson

In 1953 I left the bright city lights of Edmonton to get some legal experience. Thirty odd years later, I was still practicing in Peace River, Alberta, generally referred to as the boondocks by city lawyers. I never found any of them to be so slick that they were unbeatable when they ventured into the sticks.

For a time, I also saw clients in a small rented law office in Manning every Thursday. The office was at the back of a combined insurance office, sporting goods store and bus depot, owned and operated by Joe Buchinski. It was a good place to catch your clients both coming and going.

Manning is fifty miles north of Peace River on the way to High Level and Hay River. Originally the local citizenry had tried to call it Aurora, but some town in Ontario already had dibs on the name. As second choice, the inhabitants decided to make political hay from the provincial premier of the day, one Ernest Manning of Social Credit fame.

A gentleman of Cree extraction called Johnnie Delorme came to see me at the Manning office one day, charged by the scarlet riders of the purple plains with drunk and disorderly conduct in a public place, and resisting arrest. Naturally, he maintained his innocence.

I always kept an open mind in such matters, so my first question was, "How drunk were you, Johnnie?"

"So help me, I only had two beers!" was his indignant response.

"I might have known," I said. "Now look, if I'm going to be able to do anything for you, I have to know the truth. I've never yet found anyone charged with intoxication who ever admitted to having consumed more than two beers, even if they were falling-down drunk. In retrospect, they were sober. In fact, if questioned by anyone myself, particularly my wife, as to my drinking, I can never recall having had more than two beers, either. It's part of our Canadian tradition. When immigrants take the citizenship oath, they have to swear never to drink more than two beers at any one time. So let's refresh our memories shall we, Johnnie?"

Johnnie continued to vociferously defend his two-beer story and his innocence as I took notes. He did odd jobs for the town hotel, he said. The owner's wife operated the establishment's coffee shop and diner. On the evening in question, this lady had asked him to interrupt his cleaning in the kitchen to go over to the theatre and escort her young daughter home from a Walt Disney movie.

"I did have two beers earlier in the evening. That was it, 'cause I was working."

I interrupted. "Hold it right there. Were you with

anybody in the beer parlour? We could use them as corroborating witnesses."

"Yes, I sat down with three women who were visiting from Peace River."

"What were their names?"

"Not sure of their real ones, but they go by the names of Racehorse, Little Beaver and Stoneboat."

"Very interesting. And would they be able to verify that you only had two beers?"

"Sure, 'cause they bought them for me. I just slipped in to talk to them for a few minutes, and I remember it well for a good reason."

"What would that be?"

"Well, Stoneboat has a glass eye, and when she went to the ladies room, she dropped her eye in her beer. She always did that, to keep an eye on it, eh? Ha, ha! And so no one else would drink her beer while she was gone."

"And can the lady at the coffee shop also testify as to your sobriety?"

"She wouldn't let me fetch her darling daughter if she was in any doubt whatsoever," Johnnie contended, with logic on his side, I thought. "So I went the half block to the theatre about five minutes before I thought the show was due to come out," he continued. "I waited in the lobby. I'd only been there a minute or two when the Moundie cruiser went by. When they spotted me they slammed on the brakes, got out and jumped all over me. They dragged me into the cop car, then threw me in the cell down at the barracks. Kept me there all night."

Repeated questioning as to what conduct on his part had brought on this allegedly sudden police onslaught failed to shake his story; and if the evidence of the mother at the hotel proved to be as Johnnie stated, then there seemed no reason for the arrest and charges.

"There's something fishy here, Johnnie," I said. "Cops are like anyone else, they have their bad days and their good days, but they usually have some reason for picking up people off the street. There has to be something you aren't telling me. You're alleging they're persecuting you, not prosecuting you. Obviously they don't like you. Why?"

Johnnie grinned sheepishly as he gave up the rest of the story. The town council of Manning, in response to complaints by the citizenry about stray and roving dogs, figured the burg had grown big enough to have a dogcatcher and a pound. They advertised the position of canine custodian on a commission basis. Johnnie answered the ad and was accepted. Council designated an old shack as an animal pound and issued John with a tranquilizer rifle and some knock-out pellets for animals of various sizes.

The Manning Mounties let their resident German shepherd police dog out each evening for a run by himself. There was no record that they'd ever licensed this dog in Manning. In fact, dog licensing itself had only recently come to the town. His first night on the job, Johnnie lay in wait down the street from the RCMP building. He had old scores to settle with the constabulary, who knew him from past losing battles with booze. Johnnie had been a talented boxer in the Canadian army during the Korean war, and was not above a barroom brawl or two, just to keep his hand in.

The dog wandered by. John, a good shot, pumped a pellet into its hide, then trailed it till it passed out, then dragged the animal's body into the pound for the night. The Mounties had to pay a twenty-dollar fine to get him out in the morning. Canada's finest weren't about to forget a thing like that!

When we'd both stopped laughing, I asked, "Would you do it again if you had the chance, John?"

He thought for a few moments, then said, "Yeah, I think so." We had another good laugh.

I had lunch with the corporal of the Manning detachment about a week before the trial date. By this time, we'd entered a not guilty plea. I suggested to the corporal, "Why don't you just drop the charges against Johnnie? I think that would be nice, seeing as he's not guilty."

"Is that why we're having this little get-together?" was his first reaction.

"Come on now, Corporal, would I do that? We're just trying to keep the relationship between defence and prosecution on friendly terms."

"And why should I give him a break?" he asked.

"Well, apart from a lot of evidence that indicates his innocence, which I will gladly relate to you if necessary, let's just say that I know about the dog, you know about the dog, but relatively few people in the judicial district know about the dog. Leastwise not until the trial, they won't."

Nothing more was said on that subject and we passed on to other pleasantries. We parted company and all in all it was a nice lunch.

Came the trial date. A heavy docket, the courtroom full as usual. Johnnie's case was called by the clerk.

The RCMP prosecutor stood up and politely withdrew the charges.

And Johnnie got another freebie.

Too Minor a Matter

Hal Sisson

I was throwing darts at a picture of Pierre Trudeau in my law office one day, my reward for having tackled a difficult file, when my secretary buzzed me. A Mr. Lefebvre from Girouxville was without, she said, and desired to have words with me. She didn't say without *what*, so in the hope that it wasn't without money, I asked her to show him in.

The village cop—there was only one in Girouxville—had issued Mr. Lefebvre a traffic ticket for failing to stop at a stop sign when entering the town and coming to the main drag. He hadn't presented Lefebvre with the ticket at the time of the alleged offence. Instead, a summons to appear before the local beak had been mailed to his farm two weeks later.

Lefebvre said he'd been in town on the day in question and that he'd stopped his farm truck at the main intersection in the heart of downtown

Girouxville before proceeding across the main thoroughfare. His son was with him as a passenger and could vouch for him. The town cop had actually been leaning on the stop sign and they'd spent a minute or two in casual conversation. After this stop, Lefebvre had driven across the main street and out to his farm in the country.

"I stopped," he told me. "I know it, my son knows it, the cop knows it. I won't stand for this. I won't plead guilty. It's not justice. I want you to drive out to Girouxville next Thursday for the trial and defend me.."

While I was telling him that things are seldom just in this world and that those who get justice may not always like it, I was reading the summons. The fine for the offence was two dollars.

"You've gotta be kidding," I said. "You can't afford to defend it; win, lose or draw, I'd have to charge you too large a fee. It's too minor a matter. My advice is to just pay the fine and forget it."

"I don't care what it costs," he said in a rage. "The cop used to be my father's hired man. He's just being a smartass, throwing his weight around, showing me where the bear crapped in the rhubarb. I don't care what it costs to defend this."

"You will when I tell you," I replied, "Because all I've got to sell is time and knowledge." When I told him the amount, he shuddered and his eyes bugged out like a stepped-on toad, but he still wanted me to come. I countered that I didn't really want to go, that I was busier than a man with one hole and two rattlesnakes. It would take most of a day and I didn't really want to charge him or be bothered with his case. I was convinced his story was true, but that wasn't the issue. In the end, I told him how court is supposed to work and how to conduct himself, and that he should go there and defend himself.

"They'll put the boots to me for sure," he complained. "Between the cop and that magistrate, it'll be like going into the O.K. Corral if I don't have a gunslinger there to protect me."

But I was adamant, and Lefebvre went away disgruntled.

Came the day in May that had been set for his hearing. A beautiful sunny Alberta day, and I sure didn't feel like spending it in the office. As the morning wore on, it nagged at me that Lefebvre had been expecting something from me and I wasn't delivering, because it just didn't make good economic sense. Or did it? Certainly made legal sense. He needed help that afternoon at two p.m. Was I to be derelict in my duty as a lawyer? Did money have to enter the picture? The cops could just as easily lay a spurious charge against me someday. I told my secretary I'd be gone for the rest of the day, jumped in my car and headed southwest for Girouxville, forty pleasant backroad miles away.

I got into Girouxville about one o'clock. Typical prairie town, like all the rest from Eyebrow to Pouce Coupe: grain elevator on the far side of the railway tracks, a railway station at the head of the one wide main street that ran at right angles to the tracks. Side streets running parallel to the tracks. Girouxville wasn't more than three blocks square, the necessary shops strung out along each side of the main street, and only one business of each type.

As I drove in, I noted that the only stop signs in town were situated where the two or three side streets entered into or crossed the main street. This was an

honest-to-God one-horse town, even if the street
cleaner didn't think so. There were no horses in sight
that day; in fact, nothing moved whatsoever, no cats,
dogs or pedestrians, and of the several cars I saw, all
were parked.

I went into the small hotel, ordered a sandwich in
the drowsy coffee shop and asked where they held
court in these parts. Turned out it was a small frame
building on the north side of a side street, one block
from the main street. I parked in front of what I presumed was the courthouse. It was now about twenty
minutes to two. No sign of human presence. I waited.
Pretty soon two cars arrived, respectively bearing
what I presumed were the policeman and the lay
magistrate. They entered the small frame building
and I followed. Yes, this was the place — a bunch of
wooden chairs and a desk at the far end.

On returning to the street, I observed a plume of
dust advancing across the prairie from the west, heading straight for the courthouse. This was flat country
and you could see a couple of miles straight down the
road. The truck came on into town and stopped across
the street, several hundred yards short of the Main
Street stop sign. Lefebvre got out, followed by his son.
He was overjoyed to see me.

I told him I couldn't promise anything in this
courtroom, but I'd see what I could do. Like him, I
detected the distinct odour of kangaroo, but we would
play it by ear and see what happened.

Premier Manning had an intense aversion to
lawyers, and for years the Social Credit government of
Alberta would not appoint lawyers as magistrates,
preferring to award the jobs as prizes to local politically faithful lay supporters, henchmen, hangers-on

and bagmen. They figured lawyers to be a species like beavers, whose only ambition was to get into the middle of the stream of human endeavour and block the flow. Certainly not all lawyers make good judges, but at least they do have some knowledge of the law and courtrooms.

You couldn't say this magistrate opened court, but he did get the proceedings started. He asked Mr. Lefebvre if he had come to pay his fine. I rose and stated that I was legal counsel for the accused and that he was entering a plea of not guilty. These words seemed to aggravate, even enrage, the magistrate.

"We don't need any big-city lawyers coming down to Girouxville telling us how to run our business," he said in a stentorian tone of voice. "Furthermore, what do you and Mr. Lefebvre mean by calling me a liar with a plea like not guilty? I swore out the complaint of the constable against the accused, and I'll have you know that I am not in the habit of commissioning false documents. If Mr. Lefebvre was not guilty, I as magistrate would never have signed the summons. To say otherwise would make you in contempt of this court, and I'm going to see what I can do about that."

"I'm not trying to show any contempt for this court," I said, "I'm actually trying to hide it." He didn't seem to understand sarcasm either.

His reference to me as a big-city lawyer flattered me no end. I was more used to opposing litigants telling my clients that they would hire a big-city lawyer from Calgary or Edmonton to come up to Peace River and drag me through a knothole backwards till I looked like a ruptured duck. My city friends got a lot of business that way, and I of course didn't want to let down the side by charging any less than they did. My clients would lose face.

I finally got the magistrate settled down by pointing out that no offence was intended. It was only the
constable's alleged facts that we were disputing, and
he, the learned judge, was not personally involved. By
virtue of his position, he was only the arbiter of the
evidence that would be presented to him by both sides
of what was a difference of opinion between the town
cop and Lefebvre. Further, that every Canadian citizen, and that extended to those residing in
Girouxville, was entitled to a defence.

He seemed to have vaguely heard of this theory,
even though it seemed to interfere with the fact that part
or all of his magisterial pay came from the collection of
fines levied in his own court. Talk about your unbiased
court system. Never, ever, underestimate the power of
stupid people, either singly or in large groups.

The judge became a tad friendlier after our little
discussion. He stated that perhaps he could use a little help from someone who was accustomed to courtroom procedure. Further beating of the bush obtained
the admission that he was really at a slight loss as to
how to proceed next, as he had never before enter-
tained a not guilty plea.

I explained that the prosecution first presented
their case, placing whatever evidence they had before
the court. Any witnesses involved gave sworn testimony as to their version of the facts, and then after
this examination in chief by the prosecution, the
defence counsel had the right to cross-examine. When
the prosecution was finished, they had to say so and
then the reverse took place. When both sides were finished, they argued as to the interpretation to be placed
on the factual evidence alleged by both sides and
alluded to the statute law that pertained thereto.

When that was over, the judge, hopefully having listened carefully to it all, came to his learned decision. I didn't dwell on the weighing of witness credibility, as I figured the magistrate had already shown where he would stand on that score.

One thing I didn't tell him was that if the prosecutor also appeared as his own witness, it would constitute good grounds for a winning appeal. I already knew what his verdict was going to be no matter what happened, and I figured the cards were stacked heavily enough against Lefebvre as it was.

The cop handled his own case. He had no other choice, really. He took the stand and said Lefebvre didn't stop at the stop sign before entering Main Street on such-and-such a day. He was grinning like a donkey eating Russian thistle until I cross-examined him. When I was through, the cop was in an extremely bad mood, and the only thing he was sure about was that a dry spell usually ends in rain.

In Lefebvre's defence, his son took the stand and gave his evidence. They had stopped to talk to the police officer at the only stop sign they had encountered while passing through town. Then came the defendant himself. I had told him to play it straight and cool, not to get angry or upset, but when Lefebvre got on the stand, he laced into the cop and called him a liar and several other well-chosen epithets. The cop's face was as red as a bear's ass in saskatoon time, he was so livid with rage.

There wasn't much to argue about, although I mentioned reasonable doubt, credibility, lack of corroboration, etc. for the appeal record. The foregone conclusion occurred; the magistrate pronounced Lefebvre guilty and closed the court.

I paid Lefebvre's two-dollar fine out of my own pocket—he couldn't bring himself to do it, so I waved him outside, saying I'd handle it. When I came out into the street, the cop and Lefebvre were having a confrontation beside Lefebvre's parked truck. The cop was shouting wildly and starting to write up another traffic ticket, saying, "and furthermore, you didn't stop when you came into town today, either!"

"Hold it right there," I said, jumping into the fray. "If you're going to give him a ticket, come on back into the courtroom and write it up in front of the magistrate. I want him to see this." Surprisingly, the cop did so, and while he was at it, I was saying to the magistrate, "Can you tell me why he's doing this, because I personally observed Lefebvre approach town from the west not an hour ago and park his car out front at least two hundred yards short of the stop sign at the Main Street intersection. He hasn't moved his car, he was in court. How can he have failed to stop at a stop sign he hadn't yet come to? Don't you think Girouxville should take a serious look at this cop and his actions?"

By this time the magistrate was likely rethinking the cop himself, or maybe they were in cahoots in order to collect fines. He said he didn't know why the man was acting in such a manner, which even he had to find irrational. Obviously, not guilty pleas and court work had a bad effect on him.

I took the opportunity to inform His Honour that I would be appealing his decision to a higher court. I don't think he knew there was one. I said I'd write up the facts as I felt they had been presented, together with what had transpired in court that day, then set out my legal argument as to why the magistrate's decision should be overruled. His job, which the attorney general's department would be happy to explain to him, was to write up his version of the testimony and facts given by the parties and what had transpired in court. Then the court of appeal would look at both submissions, plus whatever representations the prosecutor and the attorney general's department cared to present.

Back in Peace River, I prepared the paperwork and filed it with the appellate court. I later had to return to Girouxville to serve papers on the magistrate. The accused, Lefebvre, was beginning to comprehend what I'd been trying to tell him all along, that it would've been far simpler to have paid the two dollar fine and expunge the cop's actions from his mind. But I now agreed with his decision not to, and kept my fee to a minimum. We'd been taught in law school, before legal aid became a racket, that every once in a while you had to do your share to help clean up the system. It took decades of effort before the Socred government of the time under Premier Manning changed its method of appointing magistrates.

This particular magistrate never did file his version of the "stated case" to the appeal court. Sadly, a shortly time later, he went fishing with friends on Lesser Slave Lake, where they have fantastic pickerel runs at times. A storm came up, the boat capsized and the magistrate drowned

But even if he had presented his version of events, nothing could have refuted the contentions of the defence, so of course the appeal was upheld.

Many months later in Edmonton, I had to personally turn up at the legislative offices of the Department of the Attorney General in order to get back the two-dollar fine. The head honcho's attitude surprised me. Typically, no matter how bad the bureaucratic end of the justice system, they don't welcome any criticism.

"For Chrissakes, Sisson, take the cheque and get out of here. What a fuss over a two-dollar fine." He was in the justice department and he didn't get the point. Not a word about the system. I guess they figured a closed mouth gathers no feet.

Lefebvre framed that two-dollar cheque. In due course of political time, the Alberta government appointed qualified lawyers as provincial magistrates and paid them a salary commensurate with their duties.

Hornswoggled by Hooch

Hal Sisson

In the late fifties, government patronage for lawyers included federal appointments to conduct litigation under the Excise Act, which covered the illegal manufacture and sale of alcohol, aka bootlegging. You were allowed to make hooch for medicinal purposes, much to the delight of some of our now leading citizenry who ran liquor into the States during Prohibition. Nowadays the peasantry can again make spirits, but only in limited quantities for their own consumption.

When John Diefenbaker got his chance to emulate the laissez-faire Mackenzie King government of Canada, I as a Tory supporter was asked to turn my back on my principles and become a crown prosecutor under the Excise Act.

The accused was a notorious bootlegger of the Peace River country, whose identity shall remain hidden to protect the guilty—alias Matt McConkey, of a small town in northern Alberta.

The RCMP had McConkey cold. They had acted on information received from a very reliable source— McConkey's younger brother Bill, who had probably sustained youthful psychological or physical wounds at Matt's hands. Either that or he wanted to take over the family business. The cops had appeared at the McConkey farming domicile and seized the evidence, which consisted of samples of the product ranging from mash to fully distilled white lightning. They took the still and all its parts, dug out from a shack that was buried under a manure pile on the back forty. Great way to disguise the odour of the mash.

Prior to the seizure, the cops had sent in an *agent provocateur* disguised as an alcoholic. Pleading a terrible need to cure a hangover with some hair of the dog, this snake in the grass offered to handsomely finance his request for medicinal aid. Matt McConkey took the bait and sold him a bottle of the best for the going price. Well, maybe only ten dollars more than he would charge a neighbour.

I took the case before I remembered that while prosecuting public benefactors like Matt, the provincial government was refusing to build a liquor store in a nearby town of about two thousand thirsty inhabitants. They did allow a permit later on, but on a lease basis, the lessor being the local member of the legislative assembly. But they didn't build the liquor store until after he'd paid for his new hotel and beer parlour.

I didn't figure I'd have much difficulty in establishing McConkey's guilt in regard to this outrageous crime. Apart from the large quantity of damning evidence, the lay magistrate was a retired RCMP officer of the fair-trial-before-we-hang-him variety. He disliked all defence counsel on general principle and he disliked me on personal principle, stemming from a long history of legal arguments between us. I had always appeared before him as counsel for the defence, but for this appearance I was technically on his side, so no problem there, I figured.

The courtroom, housed in a building that had formerly seen service as a small wood-frame church, was jammed to the rafters with locals on the day of the trial. After all, McConkey was well known in the district, disliked by some, such as the Woman's Christian Temperance Union, but a local hero and well liked by others, having supplied a much needed and appreciated service in the community for many years. His was an honestly potent product, as I was soon to discover.

The trial proceeded in the usual manner. After entering the various exhibits, I placed brother Bill, the star witness and informer, on the stand. I began his examination in chief as to the nature and quality of the home brew product manufactured and sold by his brother Matt.

The first twenty-six-ounce bottle exhibit was unlabelled and made of clear glass, through which you could see a dark red brew. Bill stated that this would have been well cut with red wine, being only one-quarter home brew.

"And how does it taste?" I asked, taking off the cap.

"It's quite a nice drink," the turncoat witness replied.

"You don't say," I remarked, taking a healthy swig from the bottle. He was right and my expression showed it. Everyone in the courtroom laughed. Even the magistrate smiled, but shook his head. You're not supposed to drink the evidence, but in this case there was lots of it, so what the hey!

The second exhibit was only pink in colour. The witness alleged this also to be a palatable drink, but twice the strength of the first bottle, likely being half wine and half home brew. When I took a drink from this second bottle I gasped and pronounced him to be correct, to the great enjoyment of the courtroom assemblage.

The third bottle was of a very light colouring, declared by Bill to be three-quarters home brew and only one-quarter wine. Anticipating my action, the crowd applauded their encouragement and I took a gulp. It seared my windpipe and sent tears running down my cheeks. I reached for the last exhibit, a bottle of absolutely clear white liquid. "And what about this one?" I asked, barely able to get the words out.

Matt's brother looked me square in the eyes and said, "I wouldn't drink that if I were you, sir. That is the pure unadulterated stuff, the real McConkey!"

But my cheering audience disagreed. I guess it's true that lawyers, particularly in the Old West, were originally frustrated actors. I should have faked it, but bracing myself, I took a swig. When that liquid fire hit my Adam's apple, it brought me to my knees. To quote W.O. Mitchell, the stuff would've given a dog's ass the heartburn. This time the magistrate's laugh was genuine. I thought I'd cauterized my tonsils; I couldn't speak, I was trembling like a dog shitting a log chain and dreading the hook.

When I was able to stand, I poured a small amount of the white lightning into an ashtray sitting on the table and lit a match to it. There was a burst of blue flame a foot high, which settled back to a flicker as the alcohol content burned itself out in the ashtray.

Regaining my speech, I quickly presented the rest

of the evidence through police witnesses: the illegal sale by Matt to the undercover cop, then the raid and seizure of the still, which had been brought into the courtroom and entered as an exhibit. I wondered where the clerk of the court would file it. I then declared that to be the case for the prosecution.

The proceedings were turned over to my learned friend Jeff Ouellette of Grande Prairie, an experienced and bilingual defence counsel. He could be tricky, and on one occasion during a civil trial when things were going poorly for him, I'm virtually certain he faked a heart attack in order to get a badly needed adjournment. He would never admit it, but his recovery time seemed nothing short of miraculous.

The magistrate asked whether Jeff would be presenting any witnesses or evidence and Jeff stated that he would not, mainly because he didn't have any. Neither had he indulged in any cross-examination of the Crown's witnesses. He couldn't put his client Matt McConkey on the stand, as he then risked cross-examination by the prosecution and charges of perjury, for which the penalty was far more severe than for a conviction for bootlegging. Jeff said he would only present legal argument. Since he hadn't presented any defence testimony, he had the first opportunity to sum up and argue the legalities of the case.

The Criminal Code and English common law say a person is innocent until proven guilty. The Excise Act literally states that the accused is guilty until he proves himself innocent. Once the prosecution has established prima facie proof of guilt, the accused has an extremely tough time proving his innocence, but it's up to him to do so, according to the statute.

Ouellette must have known of the magistrate's

predilection to convict, especially in this case where his ex-comrade policemen had put together such an air-tight case. He must have also sensed that this might be overcome by his obvious desire to shaft and embarrass the prosecutor, in this case, me. Jeff rose and he was as smooth as the inside of a schoolteacher's thigh. He stated that all of the proceedings so far had been very interesting, in fact he'd go as far as saying entertaining, but he wished to remind the court that at no time had his learned friend Mr. Sisson proven that the white liquid in the exhibit bottles was not vodka legally purchased by Mr. McConkey from an Alberta Government Liquor Store.

The defence was such a crock, so many bricks short of a load that it was no better than a tick in a lap-dog's crotch. It didn't have enough merit to pad a crutch. To attempt it took more guts than a government goat on a garbage dump. But the magistrate took the bait like a stunned jackfish in Lesser Slave Lake.

"Say no more, Mr. Ouellette," he cried out in joy, "say no more. You have hit upon the key legal point here. You have convinced the court that you are absolutely correct." Either the judge was buying his booze from McConkey or he was determined to jerk a knot in my tail, he was that happy. I didn't even get the chance to rebut. "The prosecutor not having done his job properly," and here the magistrate paused, savouring these remarks, "and having closed his case, I have unfortunately no alternative but to immediately come to my decision. Mr. McConkey, stand up. I find you not guilty of the charge."

He went on to praise the furious RCMP officers for their excellent investigative police work, which he felt may well have resulted in a conviction if only the case had been prosecuted properly. I was about as popular with the cops as a turd in a punch bowl. Only McConkey's friends and customers, who were legion, were pleased. The magistrate dismissed the case and closed the court.

Matt was borne away by the surprised and delighted crowd in a fever of jubilation. Congratulations were offered to the victorious Jeff Ouellette. You'd have thought he'd won a murder trial in Supreme Court.

I had succeeded in upstaging myself and becoming an unwitting accomplice to the acquittal of Matt McConkey. I couldn't have done better if I'd been defending him myself. Wish I could say I threw the case, but that was never my intent. Was the magistrate fair? His dislike for me was merely greater than his desire to convict, which ordinarily didn't require any evidence whatsoever in his court. Well, it was an atrocious decision in law, because the statute states that if the liquid was something other than the home brew that it obviously was, then the defence had to produce the proof of that contention.

But in retrospect it wasn't a bad decision. Matt never made the big time in the bootlegging business. He never formed his own distilling company or went on to create an eleven-billion-dollar empire. But he was making his contribution to the community in which he lived, especially in the face of government refusal to create a supply of the same product in that area for a reasonable price.

The McConkey case was the only time I acted as a crown prosecutor; at which position I have to admit that I batted zero.

Premeditated Carelessness

Hal Sisson

Trial judges often interject their own questions during a trial, but on rare occasions, they take over entirely from the prosecution. And if the accused has chosen to appear without defence counsel, the proceedings can turn into a dialogue between judge and accused. It might go something like this.

"Now tell the court in your own words, how did this unfortunate affray come to pass?"

"How did it happen, Judge?"

"Precisely. Obviously the complainant, Fred Toole, was badly beaten by someone. You are the accused, so the law presumes that you might know something about the incident. How do you plead to the charge?"

"*Nolo contendere,* Your Highness."

"Actually you can address the court any way you want, except in a contemptuous manner, of course. But nobody seems to observe the niceties anymore. Technically in this court, which is provincial court, you could say, 'Your Honour' or just 'sir.' Regardless of how you choose to address me, you have to enter a plea. Canadian jurisdictions don't allow the plea of *nolo contendere*. Do you have a lawyer?"

"No, but I thought..."

"Maybe you thought I was Judge Ito and you could just show up in my courtroom with a cockamamie plea like *nolo contendere* that's only available in the Excited States. It means that although you don't admit guilt for the record and will offer no defence against the charges, you're contesting the facts of the matter, with an explanation. That allows you the right to deny the validity of a guilty finding in any related proceedings."

"I do have an explanation, Your Honour."

"All right, let's hear it, then I'll decide what you should do. I'm doing this because you're not repre-sented by counsel. But let me advise you up front, it had better be good, because the record shows that this man, the complainant and victim, Fred Toole, has had the tar whaled out of him."

"Well, I wouldn't want to plead guilty to anything like that! Whale the tar? What's that? Maybe I do need a lawyer after all. Maybe an attorney would be able to understand these legal terms."

"What legal terms, you...you *non compos mentis*!? Now there's a term any lawyer should understand; it describes a lot of them. The expression I used, 'whale the tar,' is outdated. Let me explain in more modern terms. Do you understand the phrase 'beat the living crap out of someone?' Because that's what somebody did to this Toole guy. You can understand that? Good. So if it *was* you, let's hear why you did it. We haven't got all day, there are a lot of other people I have to find guilty today. Justice must be meted out."

"I understand. The court is where we meet justice."

"Right. But just keep in mind that when someone gets justice, they don't always like it. I'm telling you that now in case you get disappointed later. So let's hear your explanation, then I can decide what your plea should be."

"He had it coming, Your Worshipful Honour, sir."

"He had it coming!? That's it? He had it coming? You're going to have to sort of fill in the details."

"All right, Judge. Let's not get our shorts in a tangle. You see, I was in this tonsorial parlour, and..."

"Are you getting smart with me?"

"Sir?"

"Tonsorial parlour. Shorts in a tangle. Using outdated expressions on purpose."

"A linguistic anachronism, Your Honour."

"I know what you mean, but in this court call it a barber shop, or I'll cite you for something. Sarcastic contempt, maybe."

"Yes, sir. Well, anyway, I was in this barber shop. It's called *Shear Madness*, over on Main Street. It was pouring rain that day. So everyone was wearing raincoats and carrying umbrellas."

"Just a moment. The evidence in the crown prosecutor's charge indicates that this assault took place at the complainant's home. What has a barber shop got to do with it?"

"Well, this guy in the next chair, this Toole guy, and the two barbers and me, we were talking and joking and like that."

"Did the conversation have to do with this case?"

"Not really, but he did tell a couple of legal anecdotes, Your Highness, which I certainly thought were uncalled for."

"I'll just bet you did. And what was the nature of these untoward remarks about the law, may I inquire?"

"He asked us, 'What can a goose do that a duck can't do, but that a lawyer should do?' That was one thing I remember that Toole said. Anyway, I had come into the shop later than Toole had and so he was nearly through his haircut before I got started."

"Just a minute here, just hold up a second. Aren't you forgetting something?"

"What would that be, Your Worshipful Self?"

"What *can* a goose do that a duck can't do, but that a lawyer should do?"

"Well, he said that it could stick its bill up its ass, Your Honour."

"Silence in the courtroom please, or I'll have it cleared. Did Toole have any other gems of scatological legal wisdom to impart at *Shear Madness*?"

"Come to think of it, he did. I must say, sir, that Toole did give the shysters, as he called them, a very bad time. He asked what was the difference between a courthouse and a cathouse? But then he left before my haircut was finished and that was really how it all started. You see, he..."

"He left the shop before answering his own question? You're not finishing one topic before you start another."

"I thought you said I was to tell you only what happened."

"But first you're going to tell us what's the difference between a courthouse and a cathouse. My God, I'm playing straight man to this clown, I mean, the accused."

"Toole said there is no difference, sir. You can get screwed in both places."

"I've told you people about laughing in court, now shut up. So that was Mr. Toole's opinion, was it?"

"Yes, but I hope it's not true, sir."

"We'll soon see about that. Get on with it. What else did this Toole person have to say about the legal system?"

"He asked what you would call a lawyer with an IQ of ninety?"

"And what *do* you call him?"

"Well, Toole called him His Honour, the judge!"

"Order! This laughter stops or I'll cite some of you spectators for contempt."

"Then Toole said, 'How do you tell the difference between a dead judge lying in the road and a dead snake lying in the road?'"

"He said that? Mr. Crown Prosecutor, do we have the right party on trial here? Possibly you, as learned counsel for the prosecution, could enlighten us on the difference?"

"I don't know the difference, Your Honour."

"What did you say? You don't know the difference between a dead judge and a dead snake?"

"No, no, strike that from the record, please. I want to rephrase that. Actually, no comment, Your Honour, on the grounds that any answer would be detrimentally tendentious."

"So, my good man, what was Mr. Toole's answer to that little riddle? How did he tell the difference?"

"He said that there were skid marks in front of the snake! He said that just as he was leaving. He put on a raincoat and left the, ah, the barber shop."

"So?"

"So it wasn't his raincoat he put on, it was mine."

"So what did you do?"

"I noticed the remaining coat wasn't mine. They

looked alike, but the complainant had my coat instead of his own."

"Did you know who the complainant was at the time?"

"No, but his name and address were in his raincoat, so I phoned him up."

"And?"

"And I told Toole about the switch and he got real peeved and asked how long it'd take me to get over to his house with his raincoat. I said, well, I got other things to do right now, can't it wait? He said, no it can't, I have more important things to do than you have. Then he asked me for my name, address and phone number, said it's all my fault and hung up on me. His conceited condescension didn't sit too well with me but I said to myself, what the hell, I'll do it and get it over with."

"And did you?'

"Yes. I jumped in my car and drove the five miles out of my way to do it."

"Very commendable. I see you still have to enter a plea to the speeding ticket charge, which appears to have occurred on the same day. Is that when it happened?"

"Yes, Your Honour, on my way to Toole's house, but I was only doing seventy."

"In a school zone!"

"There were no kids on the street, and I was running late for my stress test at the heart clinic. When I finally got to his house—it was real hard to find—on one of those small suburban cul-de-sacs, I didn't notice the *Beware of the Dog* sign. Toole hadn't bothered to mention that to me. Lucky for me the pit bull was on a short chain, so he just got part of my leg. I wore the suit today to show the court the damage that dog did."

"That looks like it's a good suit—or was."

"A Warren K. Cook made-to-measure, sir. I know where you could get one wholesale. Well anyway, Toole answered the door with a raincoat in his hand. It was mine, all right."

"What did this Toole say to you?"

"I took off the raincoat I was wearing and he said, 'Yeah, that's mine. I'm sure glad to get it back. It's an Aquascutum, a good one. Yours is only seersucker. You must be the sucker who bought it from Sears.' All the time he was talking, he acted like it was all my fault that he'd walked out of that tonsorial parlour, sorry, barber shop, with what he called my cheap raincoat. And that's my explanation, Your Highness."

"You haven't said anything about how or why this man got so badly beaten."

"Do I have to say, sir?"

"No you don't. I think the court knows. Justice must not only be done here, but it must be seen to be done. That's my job and I have to do it and apply the law. I'm sure you understand that. Stand up. Now, I have some technical difficulties to overcome in order to accomplish justice."

"I don't understand, Your Worship."

"You don't have to, just read my lips. You wish to withdraw your submission of *nolo contendere,*do you not?"

"Well, if you say so, Milord."

"Fine. We'll consider the plea withdrawn. I find that your evidence has established a defence of extreme provocation, if in fact you did it at all. Toole did have it coming from someone, and I have a reasonable doubt in my mind that that certain someone was necessarily you. Anyone who knew Toole could have whaled the tar out of or beaten the living crap out of him. So I shall presume that you wish to enter a plea of not guilty.

"Yes, sir!"

"Mr. Crown Prosecutor, is there any further evidence to be presented to this court in support of Mr. Toole's flimsy, frivolous and trumped-up charges against this accused?

"No further evidence, sir. That is the case for the prosecution."

"Very well. In that event I have no alternative in law but to acquit the accused. On all charges, including speeding in a school zone. Further, I find that Toole's felonious actions in deliberately switching raincoats caused the accused to speed, and I accept that as a reasonable excuse. I further rule that an unknown assailant attacked and beat the living crap out of Toole, and that this was neither a mistake nor an accident. His actions and attitude clearly constitute *premeditated carelessness*, with the clear intent to get beaten up by someone. There was not only contributory negligence on the part of Toole, but I find him to be the prime causal factor in his own beating. I want his immediate arrest as an *agent provocateur*. This court is closed!"

O Canadians:
Endearing in the Pejorative

Dwayne Rowe

Canadians are the kind of people who carry travellers cheques in their money belts. Of eight professional football teams in the CFL until the mid-nineties, one of them was the Roughriders, while another was the Rough Riders. When John Diefenbaker was Prime Minister and Ottawa and Saskatchewan were squaring off in the Grey Cup classic, a reporter asked Big John, of Prince Albert, Sask., which team he was rooting for. The PM replied, "The Roughriders." Since he didn't have to spell it out—strange in itself when dealing with reporters—he was able to be ambivalent yet unequivocal, in true Canadian style.

Canadians haven't yet figured out that Florida, hotter than hell in January or Osoyoos in August, is tacky and ugly. The reason it's called Florida is that Ponce (was that his name or his occupation?) de Leon noticed the inhabitants had florid faces, florid patterns on their shirts and wandered around in the oppressive heat and humidity staring at the flora, and when asked their purpose in life answered, "Duh."

Old Ponce might've been looking for the fountain of youth, but he should take a second look at the place now. St. Petersburg, more commonly known as St. Benchsittersburg, has more funeral parlours per square mile than Victoria has hookers on Government Street. Quebeckers love Florida. They come on down by the hundreds of thousands with their *Je me souviens* licence plates (Floridians think that's French for I Make Souvenirs), congregate in bars where they consume millions of litres of Gros Mol (Molson Canadian to the Anglos) and watch Les Habitants playing something like hockey against that powerhouse team from San Jose. Their already divided loyalties were really tested when the franchise from Tampa and the Ottawa Senators, sponsored by competing mortuaries, stumbled out onto the ice.

If the NFL season hasn't ended, they watch Amurricun football, eyes glued to the twenty-five-foot screens in the taverns, afraid to move in case they miss the only punt return that year. Exciting stuff! A few remember the Alouettes winning a Grey Cup or two in Montreal, but the Miami Dolphins are the new home team.

If it's the exhibition baseball season, aka the Grapefruit League, they can stay away from the Expo games just like they do at home. Feeling guilty about not being at the fabulous winter Carnival alongside M. Bonhomme in Quebec City, they secretly (syruptiously) pour maple sugar on their grits.

Western Canadians head down to Phoenix, Tempe, Tucson or Las Vegas. Now for sheer magnificent scenery, lush and green, it don't get much prettier than that. Their diversions include gambling on keno to reduce the severity of 6/49 withdrawal, golf, bridge, drinking cheap booze and watching the nightly local news read by expatriate Canadian anchorpersons to see if their guesstimate in the daily murder pool is a winner. In the evening the fast-food joints along the never-ending commercial strips provide a thousand points of light, along with fodder that, were it not practically free, wouldn't pass anyone's lips.

The climate is apparently healthy, but once a week, late at night, the Canadians peek inside their wallet or purse, just to make sure the provincial healthcare card is still there, and hold it for a moment before putting it away. It's no accident that the number on the card is called a Social Insurance Number, or SIN, a peculiar acronym for an individual, unique identifier, which is also used when paying income tax and unemployment premiums. With luck, the kinder and gentler SINs of our generation may yet be visited upon the children.

It's also no coincidence that the visiting Canucks who eschew buying cheap cheese are still collectively known as Cheeseheads. The old appellation, Snowbirds, was kind of cute, with that great Canadian Forces aerobatic team and Anne Murray's megahit to remind us who we were.

To the Yanks and others voyaging to Canada, Calgary was a decent enough place to see during the Olympics, and a lot of visitors keep coming back for Stampede Week. Vancouver, the last time I looked, was about the best large city on the planet. Vancouver Island, especially for those sufficiently adventurous to travel north of Nanaimo, is an absolute jewel: the size of England with about 50 million fewer people and no atrocious food in the pubs like bangers and mash or bubble and squeak. Try Saskatoon in the spring, summer or fall, and head north to Batoche and discover Louis Riel. And if you haven't smelled the fresh bagels and strong coffee in downtown Montreal at seven a..m., *je le regrette*. Toronto with its lakeshore, towers, domes, subway, zoo and concert halls is fantastic. As long as we don't burn this country down, there'll be no need for anything like a Phoenix to rise from the ashes.

So Long Low

Hal Sisson

It's been nice to know ya, but so long, Solon E. Low. Not many youngsters would remember, but Low, who could talk a dog down off a meatwagon, used to be the leader of the national Social Credit Party. He was defeated by Tory G.W. (Ged) Baldwin, the most effective federal politician ever elected in the Peace River country. As a member of Ged's campaign committee, I played a small role in Low's loss, which sounded the death knell of the Socreds on the national scene.

Solon, whose parents must have named him for the sun he thought shone out of his rectum, was addicted to exaggerating the glories of Social Credit. He came from Cardston, Alberta, seven hundred miles south of where he'd chosen to run. Peace River was considered the strongest Social Credit constituency in Canada. The only time Low ever came to Peace River was just prior to elections. He spent the rest of his time in

Ottawa, unless perhaps he deigned to grace Cardston with his presence.

The Social Credit opposition in the land of Twelve Foot Davis—strangely damn few in number—figured that if Low's home-town voters wouldn't elect him, they must know something we didn't.

Why did we always allow candidates to parachute into our federal constituency? Did they think we were stupid? Solon must've picked Peace River because we formed the most ignorant part of the province of Alberta. Apparently the electorate didn't regard this as an insult to their intelligence, because we kept electing him. He had his hands in our affairs, his mouth in our ear and his faith in our patience.

That patience ran out on the night of March 31st, 1958, when the area finally elected one of its own. Solon E. was already in Cardston when the election results were officially announced. He hadn't expected anything other than the usual result in his favour again and as usual, he didn't even have the courtesy to wait to find out, let alone hold a victory celebration for his supporters in the area where he had been elected to the seat since 1945.

No, you didn't have to give Solon Low till sundown to get out of town. He always did that without being asked, this time never to darken the saloon doors of Peace River again.

The town went wild. For the first time since Alberta became a province in 1905, a resident of the area had become a member of parliament. Not only did veteran Peace River lawyer Ged Baldwin win by a margin of 11,796 to 5,094, he administered a smashing personal defeat to one of the most formidable opponents in Canada, avenging a defeat in the previous election where he himself had lost by about five thousand votes.

My most vivid memory of Baldwin's campaign team was a trip to Fort Vermilion. There was Bob Jones, Louis Sokoloski, Benny Griep, myself and Ged, and we covered places you likely never heard of, like Indian Cabins, Eureka River and LaCrete.

Take LaCrete, for instance. The place had maybe five hundred Mennonite voters, only about five of whom ever exercised their right to do so. Voting or getting involved in the political process ran contrary to their religious beliefs. At the first meeting there, I was the warm-up speaker who introduced the candidate, Ged. I was supposed to put the audience in a good mood, like the comic does for the headline singer in Las Vegas.

The site was a general store full of Mennonite elders, and I decided to try to entertain them with a little item which in magic circles used to be called a trouble wit, because if you didn't know how to operate it, well then, you had trouble wit it. The trouble wit was made of a very large piece of multi-coloured hard cardboard, folded down to about one and one half inches square and about a foot long. You could unfold it in at least twenty-seven different ways to make it look like anything from an Indian headdress to a life raft. As you did this, you told related anecdotes or jokes, or what you considered were apropos comments, in this instance related to politics.

I've suffered flop sweat a few times on stage, but this was weird. My early comic heroes had been Bob Hope and Fred Allen—how come I was performing in a general store in La Crete for fifty Mennonites? No one laughed, no one smiled, no one applauded, no one said anything. I felt like an alien from outer space. I'd rather have been nibbled to death by Canadian geese. I guess they'd never heard a person who didn't know what to say and then went ahead and said it anyway. I had never before or since seen an audience who had never heard a live comedian.

I wisely decided to cease and desist and quickly brought Ged to the rescue. They seemed to like the serious stuff better, although their outer demeanor never changed. Ged dwelled on the point that they should at least vote for someone.

Over a period of years, I know he convinced the LaCrete community that if a government office in far-away Edmonton or Ottawa couldn't tell from election results that a block of voters and a community existed in their location, then they'd pay no attention to their needs. As witness to this fact, the only paved road in the entire Peace country at that time was a short stretch of ten or twenty miles near Berwyn, running right past the home of provincial Socred MLA Lampley.

No, that's not quite true. They did say that the Main Street of Grande Prairie was paved. However that was hard to prove, because they had no street cleaning equipment and the quantity of mud that had been dropped on the street was so deep that one day a man bent down to pick up a cowboy hat lying in the roadway. Underneath he found a man's head. When they dug the guy out he was riding a horse. And the horse was on the back of a pick-up truck. I never heard that they hit pavement.

Fort Vermilion was at the end of the old D.A. Thomas paddleboat run on the Peace River, and it hadn't changed much since the last paddlewheeler hit the burg in the late forties. That was the only place where I ever attended an honest-to-God Indian Tea Dance, with drums and the whole bit. Great opportunity, and the RCMP had enough brains to remain absent. At least in uniform. One Mountie, who may have been stationed there too long, took us out there and danced in it himself, as did we.

I really don't know what kind of tea we were drinking, but it was strong medicine. The tom-toms were beating and there was dancing and stomping in a circle around the fire. The liquid refreshment was designated as plonk, and my last memory was that I was tied to a stake minding my own business at the top of my voice when I was suddenly struck drunk.

They made their own booze in that community. Had to, since the nearest government liquor store was about two hundred fifty miles south in the town of Peace River. Didn't even have one in Manning, out of deference to the premier being a teetotaler, I suppose. How's that for gratitude? They named the town after Ernest and couldn't even get a liquor store.

When the Ged Baldwin party arrived in the Fort, it was January and forty below, and the grandest hostelry was booked solid. The hotel also served as a general store, with every kind of mercantile item imaginable on the ground floor, as well as groceries and an area where eats were served to the paying customers. At the very back on the left a stairway led to the second-floor rooms that formed a single line off a hallway.

What kept you from freezing in January were the two heating units on legs in the centre of the main floor below. Each was made from two large oil drums welded together with a door built into one end.

Through this door they threw the long logs of poplar, birch, fir or what-have -you that were used for firewood. In the ceiling was a line of numbered holes, each about one foot square, through which the heat from the stoves below rose to warm the rooms above.

The system worked pretty well, except that the rooms right above the stoves could get too hot, while the ones at the ends were too cold. Also, if you got up in the long winter nights for whatever reason and forgot about the hole in the floor, you could step on air and one leg would descend through the floor up to your crotch. The result was a painful, muscle-wrenching, unforgettable, voice-raising experience.

Each room was equipped with a rope, and to get room service, customers dangled their rope through the hole in their floor and the staff would fill up a basket and tie it to the rope for the customer to haul back up. If visitors came to see you at the hotel, they'd ask which room you were in, then stand beneath the corresponding hole and yell to see if you were in.

The Baldwin crew stayed at the town's lesser hotel, the Homesteader's Inn run by Denise Eek. This was a large log edifice. The family quarters, kitchen and restaurant made up the ground floor. Ged Baldwin drew the bridal suite. It had a bureau with a cracked mirror and one beat-up easy chair in addition to a double bed.

The rooms opened off either side of a central hallway. The walls in the hallway and rooms were rough-sawn lumber covered with brown wrapping paper. The communal lavatory at the far end of the main hallway was a two-holer, two-story drop into unknown depths. I never heard anything hit bottom. Soundproofing was nonexistent throughout the building.

Benny Griep and I drew the end room next to the crapper. The bed was three-quarter size, with clammy sheets from the usual practice of hanging freshly washed sheets outside to dry at first, then bringing them inside to thaw over a line strung across the kitchen.

The next room was occupied by someone who fancied himself a cowboy singer, complete with guitar accompaniment.

Not altogether a pretty prospect as we prepared for a mid-winter night's sleep in our long johns and wool socks. I try not to think about it at all, but sometimes when I'm sleeping at the Hilton or the Four Seasons, I still remember that weekend. You had to huddle together for warmth or freeze to death.

Benny was a very proper man, so meticulous that he once learned Braille just so he could read in the dark. We had only recently met and each of us was afraid of how the other would react to this situation. Who would be the first to move as we lay there on our backs in the three-quarter bed listening to the hotel guests use the indoor-outhouse style crapper a few feet from our bed, and as we listened to the cowboy in the next room singing *My Head Hurts, My Feet Stink, and I Don't Love Jesus*? It was like an accident that you felt should be happening to someone else.

We made it through the long night and went down to breakfast at the Palace of Eats below. Denise, the owner, entered the cafe. She was a resilient woman who'd grown up on a homestead not even close to Fort Vermilion, a hardworking woman in a hard country. Everything she'd learned had come the hard way.

Denise was on breakfast duty and asked everyone what they'd like to start the day. The others gave their orders and I asked for poached eggs. She looked at me for a moment or so, then said, "Wouldn't you like to have fried eggs and bacon like the rest?"

"No, thank you," I told her. "Poached eggs, please."

A few minutes later she returned and said, "Well, if you don't want fried bacon and eggs, maybe you'd like ham and eggs?"

"No. I'd really like poached eggs on toast. I really feel that's what I would like."

Another trip to the kitchen for Denise, and a third return. "You know, a lot of people ask for poached eggs on toast, but I've always been able to talk them out of it. Truth is, I don't know how to make them, so what's it gonna be?"

"Well," said I, always willing to please, especially when on the campaign trail, "I'd be quite willing to make my own, show you how to do it."

She seemed pleased at this and ushered me into the kitchen. At first glance I figured I should have had the bacon and eggs. I was faced with a huge kitchen range—likely used to heat the entire building—on top of which, among other paraphernalia, were a couple of giant frying pans that had likely been frying eggs since the last coureur de bois passed through Fort Vermilion on his way to Great Slave Lake. These frying pans had never left their home on the range.

I gulped, picked up a boiling kettle and poured water into one of the pans, added a bit of salt, broke two eggs and dumped them into the water. She had lots of toast at the ready. Three minutes later, voilà, poached eggs on toast.

"Upon my soul," said Denise, "so that's all there is to it. I'm going to put that on the menu right away."

I suggested she buy another, smaller pan for the

separate cooking of poached eggs, so as not to interfere with the production line of bacon and eggs, which was the gourmet specialty of the house. A fine woman, Denise, who became a client and friend, and later in life became noted for her pioneer, homestead-style poetry.

Stinking Lake

Hal Sisson

No farmer can tell you where a horse's tail ends and his ass begins, but he can speak of each distinctly. Similarly, I ran as a Tory candidate in three byelections in the Peace River riding, in 1959, 1961 and 1963, and though I failed to win each time, I can speak with authority about the results. In Alberta in those days, if you said you were a Progressive Conservative, people asked why you didn't join an organized political party.

The loss I suffered at the hands of the electorate in 1961 started somewhere between Rocky Lane, where I campaigned vigorously, and Stinking Lake. I'd never heard of the latter, let alone tried to find it on a map so I could campaign there.

At Rocky Lane, ignominious defeat. The score was Social Credit, sixty-five; Liberals, five; Progressive Conservatives, one. I was staying with a university friend and his wife who were teaching school in the Rocky Lane polling station. One of them double-crossed me. Equally embarrassing, this farming area was also the one where my campaign manager had been born and raised. Even though I ran like a scald-ed cat, some people there hardly said two words to me, but they said those two all the time. I remember filleting northern pike at a fish fry to show I could do that sort of thing, all the while gulping shots of vodka and yelling "Dobra!" Man of the people sort of thing.

The whole area was controlled by an aged Ukrainian godfather, and one afternoon I was ushered into his presence for an hour's chat. Everyone was friendly and polite, as they all knew my campaign manager, Kay Sokoloski. But the godfather must have sent out the word to his troops to "Keep votin' for de old guys who are there now, dey're gonna win." The electorate of Rocky Lane were telling me I should go far, and they hoped soon. Nobody wanted to get off the gravy plane, and in those days in Rocky Lane air-craft were still horse-drawn.

Now, Stinking Lake poll was a different story — glorious victory! Tory Sisson, seven votes; Socreds, six; Liberals, three. The Stinking Lake victory was the sole maverick, lone-wolf exception for the whole con-stituency. Every other poll was won by the Ernest Manning Social Credit machine. Somewhere out there in the northern bush, sixteen votes were cast in the electoral district of Peace River, and to this day I don't know where Stinking Lake is.

I always thought I had let Stinking Lake down. I should've bought a few cases of beer and driven up to wherever it was and thrown a wingding of a party. I owed it to them for their gutsy, unprecedented support in voting against the Manning juggernaut. But I kept putting it off, maybe because having lost every other poll, plus my deposit, I also lost heart. In those days, all opposition candidates lost their deposits and Premier Manning always publicly thanked them and asked Bible Bill Aberhart and God to give them social credit in heaven for their donations to the government coffers.

The government then took an extremely un-Christian attitude regarding the drubbing they'd taken at Stinking Lake. They weren't about to let it happen again. In the next general election of June 1963, there was no longer a poll at Stinking Lake. It had vanished from the knowledge of man, and is likely only preserved in these memoirs.

Needless to say, I was shocked. What foul distemper had wiped Stinking Lake from the electoral map of Alberta? Did miasmic and poisonous effluvia arise from the noisome stenches of the swamp—it had to be called Stinking Lake for a reason—and a resulting plague lay low all the inhabitants? Was it an act of God called down by the Premier at one of his Back to the Bible Hours? Was there even a lake? I didn't know and neither did anyone else I ever asked.

The government department in charge, who was not God, but who acted for God in this field, likely gerrymandered Stinking Lake out of existence, amalgamating it with some neighbouring polling station where the Socreds had firm control of the brain-dead majority of voters. After all, a political party whose manifest destiny is guided by God cannot allow even one poll to go rotten without rendering it void.

When in the just and due course of time it came to pass that the Conservatives got their turn in the

Alberta provincial pork barrel, they didn't do any better or accomplish any more than those of whom they
had previously so bitterly complained. As Charles
Luckman once said, "The trouble with our country is
that there are too many wide-open spaces entirely
surrounded by teeth."

Those were the days, my friends, when the losing
candidates didn't have to spend a small fortune in an
attempt to get elected. Relatively speaking that is, and
allowing for the inflation factor. It still costs candidates less to run in the West.

The winning candidates in the Social Credit years
in Alberta only had to spend a small, cosmetic amount
in order to keep up appearances. They were going to
win anyway, and everyone knew it except the losers.
All it took was the "night or day" speech Ernest
Manning delivered to each constituency a few days
before each election.

The gist of the message he delivered was: "Now,
the Social Credit candidate sitting here with me in
radio station CKYL (or wherever) can walk into my
office at any time of the night or day and tell me what
you people of the north need, what you want, and
what you are therefore likely to get. I am sorry that I
cannot say the same thing about the other two professional politicians who are his opponents. If perchance
you should have the temerity to elect one of them,
they are not welcome in my office at any time of the
night or day. We don't talk to them during the day,
and certainly not at night, and if they speak to us, we
don't listen."

So much for participatory democracy in the Bible
belt of Canada, for the electorate always seem to vote
en masse for one party until they smell its defeat, at

which time they switch holus-bolus to the next group of carpetbaggers ready to feed at the public trough. The Alberta electorate didn't like to be associated with potential losers, who couldn't get them government contracts or jobs in the civil service.

However, the part in Manning's speech where he referred to candidates Wilbur Freeland and I as professional politicians—coming from a real pro like Manning—may or may not have been flattering, depending on your opinion of politicians. I don't know about Wilbur, but I've never been elected so much as dogcatcher.

Premier Manning always had a special hatred of the legal profession, which he illustrated by perpetually retaining the position of attorney general unto himself. Some detractors would say Ernest did so with good cause, and they may be right. But that wasn't our main sin in his book. We weren't Social Credit and were therefore beyond redemption.

I only know one man who actually heard Bible Bill Aberhart speak with a full head of steam, at the time when Social Credit was a new political force slithering through Alberta like a snake's belly in a wagon rut. Standing in the crowd at that political rally, Claude Campbell told me, listening to Bible Bill speak in a voice too loud for indoor use, was the only time he felt that if he challenged any of the statements that were being made or criticized any of the proposed policies, the partisan crowd would turn into a mindless mob and ride him out of town on a rail after tarring and feathering him.

This was the Dirty Thirties and feelings were running high. Any panacea offered to alleviate the Depression was acceptable, particularly when promulgated by a

preacher, a man of God. Little did anyone know at the
time that it would take Hitler and World War Two to
revive the economy.

The first time I ran for election provincially, under
Tory leader Ernest Watkins in 1959, we campaigned in
all the usual ways. We flew a small plane over all the
towns, trailing a drogue with a sign saying *Vote Sisson*.

Mel Stevenson, my campaign manager, also pulled
a lot of unorthodox stuff, not realizing a sense of
humour has a very low rating among the electorate.
Mel bought thousands of empty plastic druggist pill
capsules, made up small strips of paper, rolled them
into scrolls and inserted these in the clear containers.
On the outside, all that showed were the words, *The
Real Dope*. On the inside when you opened the capsule
and unrolled the paper, you read such messages as *A
Change is Better than the Rest.*; and *You've seen the Rest,
now try the Best*.

Mel also repackaged gum in new wrappers, which
stated *Chew Sisson—for MLA—PC Candidate*. He handed
out these items to all and sundry. Not great ideas ahead
of their time, but we couldn't have contemplated the
break-up of Canada in later years if we'd had the sense
to elect the Rhinoceros Party.

There can only be one winner in any election, but
from my own experience and observation I have
learned one true but slippery political dictum: every
government ever elected, whether it be that of your
own party or some other group of charlatans, is bound
to be worse than the last one. What else does one learn
from a failed political experience? Well, perhaps to kiss
only the babies who are old enough to vote.

The last time I ran, in 1963, was for Milt
Harradence. Harradence, a Calgary criminal lawyer at

the time, later became a Supreme Court Appellate Division judge. We had gone to University of Saskatchewan Law College together. He phoned me up and said, "Hal, can I count on you to run again this time?"

"I'd have to be so drunk I couldn't see through a ladder, Milt. We're beatin' our heads against a religious stone wall. There are no Conservatives here, not much of an organization and nobody's willing to be nominated."

"Come on now, Hal, let's not be defeatist, you can do it again."

Milt was a pilot in WW II and was now a member of the Confederate Air Force, a group of flyboys who owned their own fighter planes and flew out of somewhere in the southern U.S.

Milt flew to Peave River in his Mustang fighter plane. We met him at the airport, had a steak dinner on our patio and drove him back to his plane later that night in John Skelly's car. With us was Benny Griep, another regional director for the Conservatives. In the car on the way to the airport, the four of us held a nomination meeting and they appointed me as the PC candidate in the coming election of June 1963.

We informed the local paper, the Peace River *Record Gazette,* that an enthusiastic meeting had taken place in Peace River, a goodly crowd was in attendance and Sisson won the candidacy. The article read: "Also attending Mr. Sisson's nomination meeting was Mr. Milt Harradence, PC Provincial leader, who blasted the monolithic Social Credit policy of opposition annihilation and said that the voters of the province were beginning to see the light."

The local PC organization was broke, but the

provincial organization coughed up five hundred dollars per candidate for election expenses. This being
my third kick at the cat, I was beginning to smarten
up. I had no local organization to speak of. I didn't
place one ad, make a single speech, nor attend any
meetings. All available funds were expended on liquid
refreshments for a party on the night of the election, to
which all voters and members of all political parties
were cordially invited. And they came, candidates
and all, Liberals, Socreds, NDP and Conservatives all
mixed together, and the festivities went on till dawn.
Reputedly one of the best political bashes ever held in
Peace River.

I got the same number of votes, maybe more, than
in the previous two elections. This time the electorate
were probably rewarding me for doing nothing. I
think the voting public appreciates that. My own
opinion is that you should never elect anyone who
really wants the job, for, as Ambrose Bierce once said,
"Politics is the conduct of public affairs for private
advantage," or according to British publisher Ernest
Benn, it's "The art of looking for trouble, finding it
everywhere, diagnosing it wrongly and applying
unsuitable remedies."

Back to the Bible Hour

Hal Sisson

"One of these Sundays," Aunt Harriet warned, "I'm going to catch the little blasphemer who was singing *While Shepherds Washed Their Socks by Night*, while all the rest were singing *The Old Rugged Cross*. And when we were singing *Jesus Loves Me*, one of you boys (I know you girls wouldn't think of doing such a thing) added, *my barber told me so*. The perpetrator is going to be caught and castigated, for that kind of conduct in a church is simply unacceptable."

Aunt Harriet continued on a kindlier tack. "Now class, let us commence. The Bible story for today's Sunday school lesson is taken from Matthew, Chapter 7, Verse 1: 'Judge not that ye be not judged.' Today we are going to talk about the judgment of the Lord. You youngsters must remember that if you disobey God and your elders and indulge in saucy behaviour, you are sure to be punished. Now, you all want to hear the voices of the angels and go to heaven and not heck, don't you?"

"Yes, we do," all the children replied. All except little Willie, who remained silent.

"Don't you want to go to heaven when you die, Willie?" asked Aunt Harriet.

"Oh, when I die," replied Willie. "Sure. I thought you meant right now."

"Some of us are very judgmental of others," Aunt Harriet continued, opting to ignore the boy. "Some of us are judgmental of ourselves. But who are we to judge? That's supposed to be the job of the Lord our God on Judgment Day. That has been decided by the highest priests of religion."

Little Willie spoke up. "How did they get to be high priests?"

"A very good question," answered Aunt Harriet. "The chief of each tribe brought before God a dry rod or staff, and these rods were laid up all night in the Holy Place. The one whose rod began to grow as if it was still on a tree became the high priest. That was the way they did it in the time of Moses.   Whoever owned the dry stick, which in the morning had burst forth with green leaves and pink buds and white blushing flowers like almond blossoms, was the one chosen by God."

"My guess is, he didn't live in southern Saskatchewan," said Willie.

"Could I get to be a high priestess?" asked Clara.

"It's not very likely, my dear, but women's lib is certainly gaining ground. Now children, listen carefully to everything I say, because at the end I may ask you some questions to see how well you remember what I've told you. Now, if you looked in the Fifth book of Moses, called Deuteronomy, you could read

Chapter 1, Verse 17. But I will do it for you. 'Ye shall not respect persons in judgment; but ye shall hear the small as well as the great; ye shall not be afraid of the face of man; for the judgment is God's; and the cause that is too hard for you, bring it unto me, and I will hear it.' Now, who can tell me who is the high priest in charge of the gates of heaven?"

"St. Peter," replied Anna.

"Yes. Good girl. St. Peter is in complete charge of whether you get in or not. He will ask you a lot of questions, maybe even quiz you about the Bible. Now you have to be able to answer those questions correctly, or you may not get into heaven."

"What happens if you don't make the grade?" asked little Willie.

"There is a place called purgatory, and if you don't go straight to heck, Willie, you go to purgatory for a length of time to be decided by God. So perhaps we'd better practice answers to the questions St. Peter may ask you. I'll play the part of St. Peter. I'll ask easy questions first. How many days in the week start with the letter *t?*"

Willie thought for a few seconds, then answered, "Two."

"Yes, two. And what are they?" Aunt Harriet asked.

"Today and tomorrow!"

"Hmm. All right, answer this, you smart boy," said Aunt Harriet, by now quite vexed. "This one's a little harder. You may even need some mathematical help to get it right, which you won't have at the Pearly Gates. How many seconds are there in a year?"

A long pause on Willie's part. "That would be twelve, teacher."

"Twelve!? How do you figure that?"

"January second, February second, March second—"

"Willie, I am going to speak to you as would St. Peter. Try to have true wisdom, incline your ears to what I say. It is better to keep your mouth closed and be thought a fool, than to keep it open and remove all doubt. For God honoureth wisdom, but nobody likes a boy who cracks wise and is a smart alec. Now for my final question, which will decide whether you enter heaven or go to heck. It's simple and all you children should know the answer. Tell me the name of the Lord Our Saviour."

Willie answered immediately, before anyone else could. "Andy is his name."

Aunt Harriet closed her eyes in exasperation. "*Andy!* How on earth did you arrive at that answer, Willie?"

"The Bible and the hymn books tell me so. Andy walks with me, Andy talks with me, Andy tells me that I am his own."

There was dead silence in the Sunday school class, then a few tee-hees and titters.

"Children," asked Aunt Harriet, "is Willie going to go to heaven or heck? What do you think St. Peter is going to do? Let's have a show of hands. Willie, you've lost by one vote and must go to hell in a hand basket. Oh, you've made me say that word!"

"Is there no appeal to a higher court?" asked Willie.

"Are you by any chance planning to take up a career in law, Willie? If you are, you'll never get into heaven. You've just passed up another golden opportunity to keep your mouth shut, which you failed to take."

"But I answered all the questions correctly. I don't
see any reason to send me to hell. This is a miscarriage
of justice. This is supposed to be a democratic society
where everybody's entitled to their own opinion."

"You're not talking to a jury here, Willie. Just
remember that. In fact, if you will look up Numbers
16:10, it asks, 'And seek ye the priesthood also?' It tells
of a wicked meddler, a Levite named Korah, who was-
n't a priest, but who with pride and wilfulness, tried
to persuade people that everyone was holy and could
lead a good life and offer incense to the Lord."

"What happened to him, Aunt Harriet?" asked
Clara.

"He must have been a lawyer, a mouthpiece of
Satan, for Korah was always meddling with other
people's business and would not obey the rules as laid
down by Aaron, who, along with his sons, had been
chosen to be the priests of the tribe. Korah thought
Aaron had taken too much on himself, so Korah and
two hundred and fifty others offered incense and
praise unto the Lord, as if they had indeed been
priests and entitled to do so. God gets very angry with
those that will not try to obey those righteous and
god-fearing persons that have the rule over them, and
so He let His fire burst out and scorched them all to
death! Only the men died, mind you, not their wives
or children. After that Korah's family was better than
he had been and learned to sing God's praises in the
Psalms. The lesson we learn from this is that we must
do what God and his appointed priests want us to and
refuse to listen to false prophets and idolaters."

"Yes, and mind your own business, too," said
Willie. "But didn't I read in the Bible that Aaron was the
brother of Moses? Aunt Harriet, did that relationship

have anything to do with him becoming the high priest of the tribe? Sounds like political patronage to me."

"None whatsoever. Willie, you must have had help. You couldn't be this stupid all by yourself. I've told you how you get to be a priest already. You are a very proud and saucy boy, and your trouble is that you think a large amount of logic is going to save you from the fiery furnace. Well, it's not. My low opinion of you reflects considerable deep thought, and I hope very little prejudice. I'm not looking for trouble, Willie, but I'm willing to start some. Now let's change the subject, children."

Clara put up her hand. "I have a question, please."

"Yes?"

"What's fornication?"

"Where on earth did you hear that terrible, sinful word, Clara?"

"Well, I heard it at the Sunday school picnic, Aunt Harriet."

"From whom, may I ask?"

"From the Reverend Father."

"Good gracious child, what did he say?"

"He said, 'Fornication like this we should have had champagne, not Orange Crush.'"

"Well, my dear, you misheard him or else he wasn't speaking clearly. As to fornication, you just put that word out of your vocabulary, for I would have you avoid sin's fiery torment. There's an awful lot of fornication about and you must avoid its hot sticky tongue. Do not dally with fornication lest you be damned and will indeed go to heck."

Little Willie spoke up again. "But fornication is mentioned in the Bible, Aunt Harriet. In Revelations 17: 4 to be precise, which says, 'And the woman was arrayed in purple and scarlet colour, and decked with gold and precious stones and pearls, having a golden cup in her hand full of abominations and filthiness of her fornication.' So I figure it has something to do with sex."

"I suppose you learned that in school, didn't you, Willie? From older boys or girls or from one of those wicked avant-garde teachers financed by my taxes, which will also probably pay your university tuition as a law student. Yes, it does have something to do with sex, which is a mounting problem. If you take sex in hand you can beat it. Enough of that, now. Children, if you want to know more about the Bible, you should read the Epistles of the Apostle Paul."

"The epistles of the apostle? Why?" asked Anna.

"Because Paul was a truly great man, who, along with Saint Thomas Aquinas, several hundred years later, set the record straight about everything that Jesus meant in every one of his enigmatic statements. You have to know the rules of the game and play by those rules without squawking. Do not whine, sob, bitch or complain, just listen and obey. Now, blessed be the dearly beloved children who take this lesson to heart and heed its warning message."

Aunt Harriet paused, her eyes narrowing as she thought, Willie, you annoying rapscallion! Are you sleeping with your eyes open again? Fornication like this, I'm going to give you such a smack up the side of your head, you villainous little bastard, you'll have a thick ear for a week, so help me God! "All right, class," she said aloud, "let us bow our heads in prayer."

Willie prayed, "Our father, who art in heaven, how didja know my name? Give us this day our jelly bread..."

When the Spirit Moves You

Hal Sisson

Buck Parlee placed a personal ad in the Peace River *Record Gazette* a few years ago: 'Before I got up this morning I was thinking of the spring of '29, when you and I met for the first time near the slab shack. I have marked that place with a rock pile. Buck Parlee'.

Was Buck referring to someone still alive? Long deceased? The ad got me thinking about spiritual matters, including what happens to us when we die. Is there a spirit that lives on? The friends and lovers we lose live on in our minds, so they do have a kind of eternal presence.

The majority of what you read in the obituaries is larded with the religiosity of one faith cult or another. In North America this is usually Christianity, but as American lawyer Paul Blanchard once pronounced as his Thought of the Day, "Christianity is so full of fraud that any honest man should renounce the whole she-bang and espouse atheism instead."

The constant and continual discovery of that fraud certainly made me consider atheism. Or maybe it was when I was skipping around the radio dial and heard a religious broadcast from Toronto. The motto of the sanctimonious evangelist was, "To win the lost at any cost." He went on from there: "Let's finish up the work of Jesus, who is coming again soon. If you don't tithe and send money in to my ministry, you'll regret it. Dearly beloved, you have some of God's money!"

Now nowhere in the Bible does it say that Jesus instructed anyone to send in ten percent of their income to an evangelist. If you gave it to anyone, you were supposed to give it to the poor and needy, not the greedy. But then the Bible has seen a lot of changes, edits and even deletions over the centuries, to fit with contemporary religious beliefs. So why shouldn't the myriad evangelists do likewise, as they all chant various versions of the same sentimental gibberish you and I likely sang back when we were Sunday school kids:

> I don't care if it rains or freezes,
> I am safe in the arms of Jesus,
> I am Jesus's little lamb,
> Yes, by Jesus Christ, I am!

The man called Jesus seemed to be a man of ideas, including the idea that the soul is reincarnated after death. Any reference to reincarnation was expunged from biblical writings in the early centuries of Christianity by church officials, but then several references in the Dead Sea Scrolls, discovered in the mid-twentieth century, resurrected the concept.

In a *Frank and Ernest* cartoon, Frank asks, "Do you

believe in reincarnation, Ernest?" Ernest replies, "No. If I had lived before, I wouldn't be so confused this time around." Then there's the old joke about two wives talking: "Does your husband believe in reincarnation?" "My husband doesn't even believe in life after dinner!"

While belief in reincarnation is most characteristic of Asian belief systems, it's also a feature of the religions of pagans, Manichaeists, Gnostics and others. Many ancient Greeks held that a pre-existent soul, which they called the anima, survived bodily death and was later reincarnated in a human or other mammalian body, eventually receiving release from the cycle of birth and death and regaining its former pure state. Plato believed in an immortal soul that participates in frequent incarnations.

If I die and reincarnation proves to be true, I'll be pleasantly surprised, delighted in fact. If it's not true, there'll be nothing left of me to be disappointed.

No one knows the answer, not even Buck Parlee. Maybe he'll meet his love again near the old slab shack, but assuming she's only a memory, he's going to have to die to find out.

We all wish you luck, Buck, when the spirit moves you and you make the voyage.

Travelling in Linguistic Limbo

Dwayne Rowe

One of the most irritating aspects of travel has been
nearly eliminated by the countries in northern
Europe: inhabitants will speak English to anyone not
immediately recognized as a neighbour or family
member. As a result, travel in the Scandinavian countries, Holland, Germany, Austria, Switzerland and
even some parts of Yorkshire can be handled easily
without resorting to those infernal phrase books that
always seem to include arcane utterances like,
"Excuse me, indigenous person, need I be concerned
about diseases in the poultry?"

France has not shared in the trend, and its citizens
steadfastly refuse to speak English, or French for that
matter, to anyone whose accent doesn't identify a
place of birth within forty kilometres. A classmate of
mine toured France in the late fifties knowing only
two phrases *en français*. He was stopped by a traffic

gendarme in Paris, presumably for driving as though
his synapses were still firing. As the officer
approached, he used up one half of his vocabulary
saying, "My uncle has hemorrhoids."

"*Quel dommage*," sympathized the policeman. My
friend then trotted out the remaining weapon in his
linguistic arsenal: "Lightning has hit the postilion."
When the officer, ticket book in hand, gazed upward
to inspect any possible damage, my friend, demon-
strating the insouciance so beloved by the French,
adjusted his goggles and, with a long tri-coloured
silken scarf trailing in the wind, drove away in his
1937 MG sports car, yelling, "Long live Isadora
Duncan!" Mind you, this is the same chap who, when
visiting Friday Harbor in the San Juan Islands in the
States, insists on speaking Spanish.

If you must travel in a country that doesn't use an
alphabet you're familiar with, you do so at your peril.
In China for example, there are more than a billion
people, most of whom speak their own dialect, the
sole remaining aspect of individualism not ground
into MSG by forty years of Mao and his successors.
The common thread of these dialects is that they all
depend on precise articulation of the correct tone
when pronouncing a word.

The proper use of the tone is a bit like singing a typical Anglican hymn, but the inflection—rising, falling,
rising and falling or just plain flat, can change the
entire meaning of a word.

At one of those traditional Chinese banquets, having convinced yourself that the round, slippery things
aren't goats' eyeballs, just a form of not-yet-hard
jujubes, you decide to compliment the mother of your
host. Gesturing politely in her direction, you believe

you're saying, "Your mother appears well tonight." However, a couple of misplaced tones will have you saying, "Your horse resembles an oyster."

Apart from the difficulties inherent in the spoken language, it's impossible to read anything in Chinese. One can have three Ph.D.s and a certificate in college-level basket weaving and it's all for naught. The Asian countries use characters that have evolved from pictorial drawings and are used to represent a particular word. After thirteen years of intense study in a remote mountain village, the average Westerner can write one sentence, usually, "Get the hell out of here."

Compounding the problem, China uses Mandarin in written form, but when the intended word or phrase is spoken by someone in Guangdong province, it comes out differently. So when verbal communication fails, a Cantonese-speaking person will write out a few characters, pass it over a Mandarin speaker who will read it, chew it over for a bit, then smile and swallow, signifying the message has been fully digested.

The only equivalent that comes to mind is trying to get an estimate from a North American tradesman while pointing to your roof. If a pen and paper aren't handy, you're better off getting your dog to translate, "Ruff, ruff," and then praying the fellow doesn't take offence and run over old Rex with his sem-eye truck and squish the poor thing into the see-ment.

Or consider the case of a portly British Columbia judge, sitting temporarily in Newfoundland, who took umbrage at being addressed by a local barrister as "Your Lardship." In the ensuing written apology, the errant attorney took pains not only to spell the title correctly, but to restore calm to the judicial temperament

by assigning blame for the unfortunate misunder-
standing to the distinct dialect of that province.

The most recent study by the United Nations con-
cluded that Canada is the best place in the world in
which to live. Any primal need for exotic adventure can
be satisfied by getting an anti-mosquito shot and heading out to Alberta's Peace River Country. Linguistic
challenges can be had merely by sitting in the pubs at
night chatting with the villagers in authentic frontier
gibberish. A word of caution: just like in China, some of
the local characters are impossible to decipher.

Rank Matters

Hal Sisson

The coastal freighter's engines roared as the vessel plowed into the mounting swell of Dixon Entrance. The Pacific, whipped by westerlies, was scudded with white. The tossing deck was packed with Canadian airmen from 135 Fighter Squadron, on their way back to Canada from Annette Island, Alaska, bound for a mountaintop airfield eighty miles up the Skeena River from Prince Rupert.

The airmen had said goodbye to the huge muskeg swamp at the southern tip of the Alaska Panhandle., on which the Americans had built a runway a mile long and six hundred feet wide, to house Annette Island air base. It was 1943, and the airmen had spent six months on the base, an all but floating cluster of Quonset huts and shack-tents at one end of a crushed rock road leading through the spongy muskeg to the airstrip. There was nothing but rough water ahead of the ship, and the airmen didn't realize that they were heading for Canada's worst airport, in Terrace, B.C.

The warm air flowing up the Skeena River valley gradually chilled as it rose, then turned into fog. The sun might shine in the village at the base of the mountain, but heavy ground fog at the airport produced zero visibility. This kept aircraft on the ground ninety percent of the time, a major detriment in the unlikely event of a Japanese invasion. No bureaucrat in government was jailed, no military big shot cashiered and no politician castigated for allowing such a white elephant to be built, but I'll bet somebody and their friends made megabucks on the airport, from where gliders and slingshots would have been as effective in fighting the Japanese.

Even the supposed justification for building the airport, the shelling of the Estevan Point lighthouse by a Japanese sub, could just as easily have been a political ploy by the Mackenzie King Liberals to scare the country, particularly Quebec, into supporting conscription. The bill to institute the draft was put to a vote in Parliament a few days after the alleged shelling incident.

We'd had a squadron fund on Annette Island to pay for various services and entertainment, to which all ranks contributed. A committee ran this loosely knit organization, and I'd been joe'd to represent what were derisively termed "other ranks," a term referring to those who didn't have any rank at all, and therefore no say in any decision of import. The officers had a mess, NCOs and sergeants had a mess. Corporals, who had to take ack-ack from above, were neither fish nor fowl; they had to live with the troops, who paid as little mind to them as was possible. Common airmen had sweet essence of f-all in the way of a mess , except for the mess hall where they ate breakfast, dinner and supper. No club where they could buy hard liquor, because in theory, they weren't supposed to get drunk.

But we never ceased to try. On Annette Island, you could try to smuggle liquor in from Ketchikan, the only source of supply, but the MPs searched other ranks getting off a returning boat. They didn't search the officers, of course, so when the brilliant decision came to pack up the Hurricane Fighter Squadron's liaison operation experiment with the Yanks and move to Terrace, B.C., the officers used (perhaps purloined is a better verb) the entire squadron recreational fund to purchase booze in Ketchikan. They smuggled it onto the base, then loaded it onto the Black Ball Line coastal steamer that was to take us to Prince Rupert. The liquor was packed in wooden crates, twenty-four bottles to the case, marked *Property of Officers' Mess*.

They didn't have a meeting, they didn't ask could they do that, they didn't promise to make a bottle or two available to their "other rank" companions in arms. What they did do was pull rank—which may be why all the deep doo-doo that followed came to pass. Sure, we erks knew what had happened to the money and we knew the officers would pay it back from their Mess funds as soon as they gradually sold the contraband to themselves in Terrace. And it wasn't as if the airmen wouldn't have done the same thing themselves if they had the clout, the means or the rank to pull it off. But you can't sit idly by and let yourself be screwed, booed and tattooed.

The ship docked at Prince Rupert, a rowdy seaport during the war years. It was the only place in Canada to have an officially condoned house of ill repute, on the appropriately named Pecker Point. Civilian and military officials deemed the provision of bawdy-house entertainment for the lads to be the best way to protect the local virgins from unwanted attention.

Black market booze was selling for a dollar an ounce in the town, a high premium at that time, and there was a lot of it in the hold of the Black Ball boat. I conferred with my buddy, Fred Ryan. We weren't about to rat to either the civilian or military authori-ties, who would only have confiscated the lot for their own consumption. We decided to play it by ear to see how we could take matters into our own hands.

Stan "Hutch" Moffat was the NCO in charge of all groundcrew. He ran the squadron in the manner cal-culated to fulfill the promise made by the chiefs of staff who allegedly ran the war effort, namely, that if 135 Fighter Squadron's performance record came within the top six squadrons in Canada, we would go to the European Theatre as a unit. Under Hutch's com-mand, we came well within that parameter, but the brass double-crossed us and the transfer never hap-pened. Another grievance stored up by every man in 135 Squadron.

Well, Hutch called for a retard party of twelve ground crew to stay behind in Prince Rupert to unload the ship, while the balance of the personnel were transported by train to the squadron's new post-ing at the Terrace station.

Huge booms lifted the cargo from the steamer's hold, swung it over to the dock, where it dropped the equipment and crates onto trolleys. These were trun-dled through the freight sheds to the railway lines, and the whole conglomeration was loaded into boxcars for transport. Contrary to our usual modus operandi, Freddie and I were the first to jump up and volunteer for this labour-intensive opertion.

We recruited four other airmen we thought we could trust, Bobby Cochrane being one name I remember well. We watched for anything labelled *Officers' Mess*, and any crate that looked like it might be packed with bottles of booze. Each freight car was sealed as it was filled, so when we found a likely-looking crate, a couple of us had to make sure it was kept moving forward from boxcar to boxcar until it arrived in the last car we would be filling at day's end. That last boxcar wouldn't be sealed that evening, but completed the following morning.

We came back that night, of course, dressed all in dark blue. Our commando training finally of some use, we enlarged a hole in the perimeter fence of the railway yards and moved in on the freight car. We liberated three crates we'd spotted earlier, then pried them open under a railway trestle over the saltchuck, dropping the boards and packing into the flotsam and jetsam drifting beneath us on the ocean tide.

Bonanza! Twenty-four bottles of whiskey in each crate: scotch, gin and a mixed bag of Old Orchard bourbon and Southern Comfort. Twelve twenty-six ounce bottles each, eighteen hundred and seventy-two ounces in all, worth eighteen hundred and seventy-two bucks, a considerable sum when you were making a dollar thirty a day. We loaded the bottles into the knapsacks and duffel bags we'd brought for the purpose and marched circumspectly back to the Seal Cove RCAF station. Each man stashed his share wherever he felt it was safe from detection. This time we were really farting into silk, or so we thought.

Now came the tough part. How much to consume and how much to sell? We weren't going to be in Seal Cove long, so most of us decided to drink some right away and sell the rest, then use the proceeds to buy beer in the local beverage rooms and beer parlours.

There was little else to do in Prince Rupert at the time. You couldn't even chase the local women—any that weren't hookers were kept under lock and key or strict surveillance. You could maybe stand outside a convent and yell "Anybody want to quit?"

Being very flush with ill-gotten gain, Fred, Bobby and I got thoroughly inebriated in a downtown beer emporium, even spreading our largesse by the purchase of the odd round for our comrades, including the navy. We figured they'd be less liable to pick a fight with us that way. We could afford the luxury of a cab back to camp at Seal Cove.

It was the middle of the night when we entered the mess hall. The graveyard shift was preparing the basics for various meals of the next day. We were ravenous, having felt no need to eat earlier when restaurants were open in downtown Rupert. We asked to be fed.

No dice, said the cooks. We thought it'd be nice if they allowed us an early breakfast. They told us to get stuffed. We demanded some sustenance as a matter of human rights and/or compassion for the starving.

The cooks asked where we were from. We told them we'd been in the bush for six months and had only just arrived back in so-called civilization.

The sergeant in charge didn't say, "Then why don't you seek transportation back to the bush?" etcetera. Let's call a spade a spade. He said, "Then why don't you just fuck off back to the bush where you belong?"

There it was again—the arrogant attitude of someone

ordering around those of lesser rank and therefore, lower status. Very off-putting.

That's when Freddie grabbed a pie from behind the counter and blindsided the sergeant in the head. The fight was on—there was more throwing of any edible item that came to hand, there was cursing, wrestling and general pandemonium, until some smartass cook put in a call to the guard-house and the military police.

We heard or sensed they were coming and high-tailed it from the scene with the MPs in hot pursuit. I ran over coal piles, around hangars, through Quonset hut barracks housing sleeping airmen. I spotted an unoccupied bunk, jumped in and pulled the blankets up around my head as my pursuers thundered past and out the other end of the hut. I had escaped. They caught Bobbie Cochrane but not Freddie Ryan, who had started the ruckus in the first place, but then Freddie always seemed to lead a charmed life.

In the pink dawn I made my way back to my own bunk. Worry is interest paid on trouble before it falls due. Later, on the way to the mess hall for breakfast, the realization dawned that I was a wanted man. A notice on the bulletin board described the culprits sought by the enraged authorities. I was characterized as "a curly-headed cunt with a moustache." The military police have never been known for their erudition, but the blatant bullshit in the notice hurt my feelings, offended my sensibilities and caused me to shave off my moustache. The rest of the description was beyond my powers of alteration.

You could stay out of traffic, but the air force station wasn't an easy place to hide, and a day or two

later a cook spotted me and squealed and I found
myself in the digger with Bobby Cochrane.

We got a hearing before the commanding officer of
Seal Cove station. A sergeant marched Cochrane and I
before the CO, whose mood was so ugly that flies
wouldn't have alighted on him if he had been covered
in excrement.

With an expression of mixed hostility, impatience
and superiority on his long-nosed face, he asked a
provost corporal to read the charges against the
accused.

This the corporal did in a high-pitched, nasal voice:
"The accused, R149662, Harold Sisson, and R142797,
Robert Cochrane, on strength of 135 Hurricane Fighter
Squadron, Royal Canadian Air Force, are charged with
the following: when on active service, they did wilfully fail to obey the order of a superior officer, namely
Sergeant Meaney, and when told to remove themselves
from the premises of the mess hall"—and here he
stopped for breath, then rushed on with the rest—"the
accused did proceed to wilfully destruct air force property while drunk and behaving in a disorderly fashion..." The corporal recited the detailed litany of our
various alleged crimes.

We pleaded not guilty because you never know
your luck. In the military they could charge you with
just about anything if they felt like it, including something called "dumb insolence." In this instance we
were guilty of the lot, so what could we say?

I tried defences like failure to provide food, airmen
for the use of, sufficient to sustain life and undue and
insulting provocation on the part of the cooks.

"Which one of you called the cooking staff a bunch
of bastards?" asked our judge.

Bobby replied, "Who called that bunch of bastards cooks?" and our fate was sealed.

But in the end, we were saved by a technicality. The judge, a crusty old SOB of about thirty-five years, probably an accountant in civvy street, accepted the charge as read, not even bothering to call prosecution witnesses. He ruled that he knew we were guilty just by looking at us. However, as we were members of another RCAF unit, we didn't come under his jurisdiction when it came to punishment. He had to send us to the Terrace station for sentencing by our own commanding officer.

Saved by the bell, for this paragon of virtue also said, "You are indeed lucky, because if I was in charge of your punishment, I'd throw the book at you. If you ever have the misfortune to be posted back to this station, you'll wish you were dead." I was convinced he meant it. Talk about no sense of humour.

Bobby and I were sent by train, with an armed guard to boot, up to Terrace. The rest of the retard party was on the same train, including Freddie Ryan, who once again had escaped detection.

The Terrace hearing took place shortly thereafter. Solemn, but not the unfriendly atmosphere so much in evidence at Seal Cove. After all, we knew these guys, they were our comrades. The CO of 135 squadron was Bud O'Connell, at twenty-four only a couple of years older than ourselves, a survivor of the Battle of Britain, a legitimate hero and worthy of our admiration. He wasn't going to make too much of a fight by some of his men in somebody else's mess hall.

I had been up on charges before Bud O'Connell on previous occasions, for a relatively minor offence. I'd been home to Moose Jaw for Christmas, and had, I say inadvertently, overstayed my leave, arriving back for duty two days late. This was never tolerated by the forces and was literally indefensible for any reason. The severity of the punishment depended on the circumstances, the length of time you were AWOL and the mood of the judge. The facts in this instance weren't in dispute and the usual routine took place. Bud asked if I had anything to say before sentencing. Were there any mitigating circumstances?

"Well, sir, on my way home I'd made a date with a very attractive young lady of my recent acquaintance. It was for the Saturday of my return to Vancouver. We were going dancing at the Cave, and I had high hopes of this date extending throughout the weekend. When I more thoroughly scrutinized my leave dates and train travelling schedule on the CPR, I found, to my horror, sir, that I was supposed to be back here on the selfsame Saturday. I'd stupidly thought it was Monday I was to be back. Well, what was I to do? I could either catch the ferry to Victoria and report back to camp on time, or I could spend the weekend with what I figured was a hot date in Vancouver. I have to ask you, and would like you to consider in mitigation—what would you have done under the same circumstances?"

O'Connell's expression didn't change, he just sat staring at me.

"I sort of felt I was upholding the honour of the squadron in refusing to break the date with the lady. And I really didn't think you needed me here—very badly, that is—over the weekend..." my voice trailed off.

"I know your type, Sisson," Bud said. "I should punish you severely. However, it also happens that 135 squadron has received great news in your absence.

We've been posted to Alaska to provide more air power for the American forces. We leave in a few days."

"This is great news, sir," I chimed in.

"And this afternoon," he continued, "there's a squadron barbecue and beer-fight down on the beach. I'm sentencing you to one day in the digger, but I'm releasing you into my custody for the day. You will report to me at two o'clock this afternoon, which is when we depart, so I can be sure you haven't gone AWOL again. Dismissed!"

It was a great party. One would never have known that beer was in short supply due to rationing, and O'Connell could put it down with the best. The entire squadron, all ranks, were drinking together in and out of the ocean. When Bud got one over the eight, and I being released to his custody, he issued a challenge: "Sisson and I will wrestle any two of you!" Oh, damn it, I found out what he meant when he mentioned severe punishment. It was brutal but fun, and we did win some matches.

Given our history, I wasn't exactly heartbroken to have the Seal Cove charges re-hashed before Bud O'Connell, although we realized he wasn't liable to be so lenient on this occasion.

By this time the officers' mess knew they were short three cases of booze. They knew we'd been on the retard detail in charge of loading, and we'd been drunk at the Seal Cove mess hall. Only circumstantial evidence of course, and no one had found liquor in our possession, but it was very suspicious nonetheless.

As usual, they removed our caps and belts—the latter so you couldn't hang yourself from fear or remorse at having sullied Her Majesty's trust in you—and marched us before the CO's desk, where we stood

rigidly at attention throughout the proceedings. Sure
was nerve-racking.

The charges were read out again, with the adjutant
reading out the details of crimes as forwarded from
Seal Cove. He then began examination in chief in
order to get out the details. "Were you drinking?
Where? Why did you go to the mess hall?" Then we
came to the ticklish bit. The adjutant became impa-
tient, and asked the question on everyone's mind, "Do
you know anything about some liquor missing from
the officers' mess supplies?"

"What liquor would that be, sir?" I innocently
asked.

"Bottles of liquor which I am informed were with
the equipment and supplies brought down from
Annette Island," the CO interjected.

"In the hold of the Black Ball Line steamer? Is that
what you're telling me, sir?"

"That's what I've been told, airman. And that some
of it went missing. Do you know anything about it?"

"Am I being given to understand that there was a
supply of contraband liquor being smuggled into
Canada from Alaska by the officers of 135 Squadron?
This would certainly be news to me, sir, that they'd
even think of doing an illegal thing like that. I can't
bring myself to believe they did!"

A pause in the proceedings, then the adjutant called
for an adjournment. They all retired to the adjutant's
room, separated from the CO's office by a double-
glazed window. From where Bobby Cochrane and I
stood we could see them all in earnest conversation,
including Bud the judge. I never liked it when the
judge and the prosecutor had a private conversation
during a court case, and the accused, who doesn't

have a lawyer, wasn't present. Seemed to leave something to be desired by way of fair trial, but then maybe someone in that conference was arguing in our favour.

They returned and the trial proceeded with no further mention of missing liquor. Net result—we hadn't caused any trouble in our own outfit, the matter of the booze was not properly a matter before this court (they couldn't nail us for the missing whiskey without implicating themselves), so they were hoist on their own petard.

On the matter of the Seal Cove brawl, the verdict was still guilty. We were confined to barracks for thirty days, with extra duties each weekday under the guidance of the MP detachment.

Fair enough; there was nothing to do in Terrace in mid-winter anyway. You were literally up a foggy mountain without a prayer, twenty miles or so from a town of a few hundred people, with a thousand Canadian army troops in a camp next to the village. There was one hotel with a beer parlour and restaurant. There was always a line-up in front of the ten-by-twenty shack that served as a liquor store, and on paydays it stretched for several blocks until the short supply of booze ran out.

As it turned out, there was something for us to do after all. An MP corporal saw to that when it came to the extra work we were assigned every day. There was little flying and nothing to do at the armament section, so Bobby and I and other airmen guilty of some misdemeanour or other were paraded every day to do whatever work was required on this brand-new station in the B.C. mountains. Not for us the usual bubble dancing and pearl diving in the kitchen wash-ups.

Coal provided the heat for all the station's needs,

and a mountainous supply of coal chunks had been dumped on the paved square in the motor vehicle area. At one end of the paved lot was a line of open-faced weather shelters for the three-ton air force lorries. A roof over their bonnets as it were, and the open front end would ordinarily have allowed the standard-width trucks to pull in under this cover. But the coal was piled so high in front of the shelter, it spilled down and half-filled the long shed, flowing between the many twelve-by-twelve pillars along the front of the building till it was six or eight feet deep.

To top it all off, the posts had been built too close together for the lorries to fit, even if it weren't for the coal. The whole situation had to be corrected, and the corporal was in charge of the manual labour that was going to accomplish the task. It was time to drop your cocks, grab your socks and start to shovel coal.

I don't know who started the next fiasco. It wasn't me; I figured I was in enough crap already, and could do with a little less. Ordinarily, like all prisoners, we worked as slowly as possible, all the while joking and passing the time of day, with a lookout posted to warn of the corporal's approach. Being lazy himself, he recognized the trait in others, so he had an idea of how fast we worked and didn't come around too often to check on us. When he did, he'd either revile our ancestry or scoff at our low and dirty coal dump estate.

The corporal had said, in a rather loose fashion, that when the coal was removed from inside the open shed, that the posts also had to be removed, because they were too close together. He may very well have meant the removal of every second post, but our collective memory was that he said the posts were too close together and had to be removed. Superior offi-

cers didn't like to explain; you were just supposed to
shut up and obey their orders.

The corporal had just cursed us out and left the
scene for either a long coffee break or his bunk, when
someone started to work at top speed for a change,
and this strange action seemed to infect us all. A fit of
madness swept through the little chain gang of prisoners. We worked till the sweat soaked our coal-
stained coveralls, we lifted and carried the big lumps
and shovelled the small as fast as we could.

When we'd cleared the majority of the coal from
the open-air garage, we took the axes and saws the
corporal had provided and cut down every last post
except for the ones at either end. By the time the corporal reappeared, the roof of the building had already
begun to sag in the middle.

"Jesus Christ!" he blasphemed, in a paroxysm of
fear and anger. He was shaking so bad he would've
had to use a funnel to stick his finger up his ass.
"What in hell have you done?" he shrieked.

"Just following orders, Corp," someone said, "isn't
that what you wanted?"

"You stupid sons of bitches, you, you ...," he was
having a conniption fit.

And well he might, because the situation was now
really serious, for him as well as us. This was destruc-
tion of government property. Never mind that the
vehicle shed should've been built properly in the first
place, and that the parking square should never have
been filled with coal, there was major expense
involved here.

Every one of the participating prisoners was
placed on charge, including and particularly the corporal. If he'd been a warrant officer or a flight looey,

his rank would likely have saved him, but as a corporal his rank wasn't high enough to protect him. He wasn't actually charged initially until the unanimous evidence from the accused airmen showed that it was the corporal who had ordered the deed done. Our superiors likely figured we were stupid enough to have done it, but incapable of consciously planning such a senseless action, so they sacrificed the corporal. He lost his stripes and did some extra duties of his own and had to move into airman's barracks again. Did we feel sorry for him? As one of the chaps put it, our parents could have shown the ex-corporal something that his own could not—a marriage certificate!

A Dog's Tale

Hal Sisson

In the mess hall at the RCAF base in Mossbank, Saskatchewan during WWII, the food got so bad the airmen stationed there launched a general strike. The strike was actually sparked by the air force's attempt to charge the servicemen extra to upgrade the food.

'Happy is the day when an airman gets his pay' were the words of an old service song called *I've Got Sixpence*, but not if something was going to be deducted from his measly dollar thirty a day.

When the strike began, the officer of the day came into the mess hall accompanied by a warrant officer and asked, "Are there any complaints?"

One foolhardy airman spoke up. "Yeah, not even a dog would eat this food."

Spotting a dog passing by the door, the warrant officer whistled the animal into the mess hall. Taking the airman's plate of untouched food, he put it down in front of the dog. The hungry mongrel wolfed it down.

"There, you see? A dog *will* eat the food served here," said the officer.

"Yeah," the airman shot back, "but look at him now. He's over there licking his ass, trying to get the bad taste out of his mouth!"

Lottos: Where Losing is a Safe Bet

Dwayne Rowe

Lottos. From the Greek, meaning Island of Losers. Like millions of Canadians, I participate in lotteries, even though I know they truly are a tax on the stupid. Why do I buy them when I can go weeks without one correct number? I even play something call the Extra, which means I'm extra stupid.

I come from a long line of non-winners. My grandfather inherited a pumpkin farm in Sweden and the government of the day promptly cancelled Halloween. There have been tell-tale signs throughout my life that Lady Luck was really Leona Helmsley. The Littlest Hobo (theme music swelling in the background) once rescued my neighbour Horst (by profession a German shepherd) from a burning house. At this point in the story, the loveable canine usually lopes off into the sunset barking Arf Wiedersehn, but this one returned the next day to poop on my lawn.

Juan Valdez arrived at our house one morning without so much as a by-your-leave and spit in my Colombian coffee. He did have the decency to leave his burro outside, but that critter ain't yard-trained, either. Despite the tremendous boost to the growth of our prize roses, if my wife ever sees old Juan again, she's going to kick his ass.

The only time I ever won a draw was in Calgary at the annual Italian community dinner. The crowd was hushed as a hand reached into the barrel. The draw master peered at the ticket, then called my name. The only non-paisan in the crowd, I won twenty pounds of tortellini, hand rolled by Calabrese grandmothers. A swarthy man from New Jersey presented the prize and kissed me full on the lips.

I tried Sports Action betting. This is the game in which the government acts as the bookie to handle the few dollars it hasn't previously extracted from you. The idea is to bet on the outcome of three, four or five games of different kinds, like hockey, soccer, basketball or dodge ball. The trick is, you have to get all of them right to win.

The problem is that San Jose could tie or even beat Montreal on the same evening in which it rains in California for the first time in thirty-seven years. The Manchester United star forward could pull a hamstring in morning practice, but with the time difference, West Coast people would literally be in the dark. So you make a hefty bet and the resulting score is a 1-0 drubbing for your chosen team. Hence the derivation of the term Greenwich Mean Time.

The lottery people keep devising new games. In the old days, the Irish Sweepstakes tickets were highly desirable, and illegal. People bought them from local pushers, using pseudonyms like Big Charlie or Dolly P. It was considered a sin to participate, thus a daring and slightly salacious act.

Before Big Brother opened up shop, the Mafia ran the numbers racket, the winning digits coming from the daily boxcar-loading totals at the Winnipeg grain terminal. The Mob returned about eighty cents on the dollar, about double what the government now pays. What was illegal back then is not only legal now, it is a citizen's bounden duty, after watching the ads on the tube, to bust open the piggy bank, run down to the convenient corner store and line up to be a loser.

The games of chance are highly specialized in order to appeal to the most arcane special-interest group. For example, dermatologists can play Scratch and Win. Profits go to a fund that is then distributed in the form of grants to equally obscure groups participating in some form of recreation they never cared enough about to pay for out of their own pockets. The local MLA is photographed grinning like Knowlton Nash on Valium, handing over a cheque to the president of the Estonian North Island Polo Federation, beaming astride Riga's Joy. The recipient later remarks to the politician that it must be a new experience to be in the company of an entire horse.

The only thing worse than losing would be to win a humongous six-million-dollar jackpot. The theory of relativity would rapidly be demonstrated as a thirteenth cousin, now selling mutual funds for Greater Rock of America Western Growth, appeared with the wife and kids for a visit. One would be inundated with pitches for everything from cars to swimming pools to pleas for investment in goofy business ventures. The only solution would be to piece off the kids quick, then blow the rest on half a duplex in the high-rent district.

A buddy of mine got five numbers right on the 6/49 and picked up a cool two thousand Lotto dollars. He went out the next day and bought a self-propelled lawnmower with bells, whistles, gizmos and a digital read-out instrument panel. He pushed the instant electric start button, adjusted the throttle, put it in gear and began to trim the lawn to precise, laser-guided measurements. While watching the torque-to-rpm ratio gauge, he ran over his foot. He took a couple of weeks off work and went on a healing retreat. To the Island of Lottos.

Doin' the Varsity Drag

Hal Sisson

In the years following World War Two, Canadian veterans received sixty dollars per month, plus free tuition at colleges and universities, for as many months as they had served in the armed forces. Many vets used their benefits to obtain a professional university degree. Because the vets were older students, their professors were often among the youngest in the classroom. Personally, I hadn't been older than the teacher since grade school.

Professor Bert Peebles, whose teaching schedule included a half class in labour law during my final year at the University of Saskatchewan Law School in Saskatoon, found himself junior to most of his students. Bert was a nice young guy, a brilliant student, who didn't put on any side, despite suddenly attaining professorial status. His voice had the unfortunate tendency to break into a higher pitch, especially when he became agitated. He was conscious of the greater

age and life experience of some of his students, and
that many of them had recently commanded aircraft,
ships, tanks and troops. I got along well with
Professor Peebles, often riding the streetcar with him
to the university. Outside of class or at social functions, the students treated him as a peer, with the deference due to a professor.

Labour Law was held in a long, narrow room with
windows down one side and a centre aisle flanked by
double-wide desks, enough to seat thirty students.
The wall behind the prof's desk held a blackboard and
the only door to the room was beside Peebles's desk.

The class generally started with a discussion of the
legal cases Peebles had assigned for study. He'd pick
someone to read out a detailed analysis of the facts,
judgment, legal principles and conclusions to be
drawn from each case.

"Would you please read the case of *O'Lofflin v.
Scudmuffler Trade Union*, ah, Hal," said Bert one day. I
had not previously reviewed the case, so I decided to
wing it. I grabbed the open notebook of my seat partner, Dave Darby, and quickly perused the headnote.

"The facts revolved around a bitter disagreement
between the union and one of its members, one Stash
O'Lofflin, who subsequently sued the union for
wrongfully blackballing him from their ranks.
Apparently the union felt that the plaintiff, O'Lofflin,
was loose as ashes and twice as shifty."

A bit of laughter from the class.

"Just give us the facts, Hal, and forget about the
similes," said Bert.

"The plaintiff, O'Lofflin, contended that the defendant union had falsely accused him of wrongdoing and
that when they couldn't confirm their circumstantial

evidence, they commenced a campaign of personal harassment. The Scudmuffler Trade Union pursued him like a fart through a keg of nails."

A few more chuckles from the class.

"Mr. Sisson, please stick to the facts and the judicial finding in this case," Professor Peebles said in a louder voice, which had taken on a higher pitch. "We want a serious attitude in this class. Enough of that kind of descriptive language."

Guffaws from some classmates, sparking an irresistible impulse in me to continue in the same vein.

"Yessir. Well, it seems that the union wouldn't have minded so much if the plaintiff O'Lofflin had been wasting either the public or the employer's time and money, which was a usual and accepted fact, but they took great exception to his adopting the same work methods and attitude when it came to union business. They tried to entrap him, but O'Lofflin proved as elusive as a shithouse mouse. Said plaintiff became as anxious as a long-tailed cat in a roomful of rocking chairs. He had a nervous breakdown and sued the union."

Huge laughter from the class. By now, the prof's voice was squeaking as he commanded, "That's it! Enough! You can stop reading now. Mr. Knechtel, would you read what you have in your notes on this case."

I figured that was the end of a mildly amusing incident. Two days later we had our next Labour Law class. I entered the classroom, walked down the centre aisle to a seat near the rear and sat down. When I looked forward, I saw that someone had written on the blackboard, "No Humour Allowed in this Class, Just Write Down What I Scream at You in a High-Pitched Voice and Memorize It!"

The sheep had hit the fence!

I started back up the aisle as fast as I could, pushing past incoming law students, but just as I got clear, Bert Peebles came through the door, already able to read what was on the blackboard. He looked at me. It must have appeared that I'd just left the blackboard. I turned and tried to grab a seat, hoping the blame would fall on the whole class and not only on me.

Bert's face went deathly white and contorted as he proceeded silently to the blackboard and rubbed out the offending words. I got back to my seat as Bert turned to face the class, the pallor of his face shifting to purple rage. He said nothing about the blackboard message at all, just started the class as usual. The class remained silent and the hour passed in the solemn study of labour law.

What to do? The circumstantial evidence, from Bert's standpoint, was irrefutable, all pointing to me. It reminded me of the story of the woman who baked a delicious pie. She had to leave the kitchen for a while and told her son, "Now don't touch that pie. We want it for your dad's dinner tonight." No sooner had she left the room than the kid dipped into the pie and ate a big chunk. He heard his mother coming back. He grabbed the family cat and rubbed its face in the pie. The mother returned to see the pie in shambles, with fruit and crumbs plastered all over the cat's face. When the father came home, she told him about the dessert fiasco. The father was furious. He dragged the cat out to the barn by its collar, and the next sound the kid and his mother heard was a gunshot. "Poor kitty," the kid said. "Another victim of circumstantial evidence."

I stood convicted, as the blackboard message obviously referred to my previous classroom antics and

Bert thought I had written the doggerel. I didn't know who had done me in, but I paid the price. You don't hold a man up to public ridicule and expect not to make an enemy. Bert refused to talk to me about it or listen to my protestations of innocence.

It wasn't as if I didn't know the necessary amount of labour law. The notes kept by students from previous years were of approximately the same content, some being prepared better than others. I had gathered together several of the best and compiled a complete set of notes on the class for my own benefit. I was also selling the set to other students for five bucks a copy.

I studied hard for the exam. When you write an exam, you always know whether you did well or poorly. I knew I would have to do very well indeed and I thought I'd done so. I perused the published marks and saw I'd failed labour law. I didn't graduate with my class and had to write a supplemental exam in the fall, which I passed. I guess Bert wasn't that mad, or someone else had marked the second paper.

It was two years before I found out who did it. Red Waldo had written the fatal words on the blackboard, but by then it was the proverbial water under the bridge. Well, if you live by the joke, you can die by the joke.

Red had his own problems. Despite what people think of lawyers, there's a lot of stress involved in the profession, which is often alleviated by resorting to alcohol. Red purposely drank himself to death in his forties.

The Sham Interloper

Hal Sisson

In the fall of 1946, the University of Saskatchewan's main campus was crowded to capacity by returning veterans, so campus authorities pressed the RCAF Airport north of the city into service for the overflow students. The College of Commerce and some arts and science students were assigned to this location, and many student vets were also housed in the Quonset huts formerly occupied by airmen. Not much change in the surroundings for veterans. The shift of location meant we didn't often frequent the main campus that year, so we didn't quite feel part of the standard varsity scene.

The Freshman's Ball was the big dance that kicked off the year. It was held at the exhibition grounds hockey arena, the paved ice surface serving as the dance floor, and most of the students attended. At that time in Canada's weird history with alcohol, there was no provision for a bar, so just soft drinks, coffee and foodstuffs were offered. If you wanted a beer or a hard drink, you had to bring your own, which theoretically made nearly everyone a criminal if they got caught. Those who wanted a libation had to partake in their cars or in the stands or tipple surreptitiously out of flasks. A lot of thought must have gone into that great system. The government hadn't learned a thing from Prohibition.

A group of us from the airport campus went to the dance heavily laden with a suitcase full of beer, which we cached high in the seats opposite centre ice, where we would repair occasionally for liquid refreshment.

The only palatial seating was a group of chesterfields and easy chairs grouped in one corner of the dance floor, reserved for the professors who were acting as chaperones. In perambulating around this makeshift *palais de dance*, I noticed a lone lady on one of these large divans. Considerably older than I but handsome indeed in an austere way. I asked whether she'd care to dance. She did and we merged into the crowd on the cement floor.

Some general polite conversation ensued regarding the band, the turnout, the price of coffee beans in Brazil, whatever.

"What faculty are you in?" she asked.

"I don't follow you," I said. "Faculty... faculty? I'm not familiar with the term."

It was a university dance and she was surprised at my ignorance of the basics. "The college in which you're registered. What are you studying at the university?"

"Oh, this is a university dance?" I asked. "Yes, I just got here, and I was beginning to think it must be something like that."

Her attitude changed slightly and she switched to an authoritative mode. "Do you mean, young man, that you're not a student on the university campus?"

"Well, no, I'm not, not actually, no."

"Then may I ask what you're doing at this dance? It's strictly for university students, you see."

"I'm a travelling salesman, ma'am. I was passing by and I saw all these cars, heard the music—it looked like a good dance, so I came in. I saw you and you're the first person I've danced with; and I'm certainly enjoying it."

"I'm sorry, you said your name was Hal? Yes, well I'm sorry Hal, but this dance is the Freshman's Ball for university students only, and I'm afraid I'm going to have to ask you to leave."

"Hold the phone a minute. Your name's Edith, right? You don't really mean that, do you, Edith? I mean, I just got here and we're just starting to have a good time. I don't mean to be impolite, but how can you kick me out, anyway?"

"Because I'm Edith Rowles, the Dean of Women. It's nothing personal, you understand, because you seem to be a nice young man, but we have our rules."

"You mean you have to protect all these young ladies from travelling salesmen? That's a big job. Can't be much fun."

"It's not supposed to be. So let's finish this dance, and then you should leave and go wherever else you think is appropriate."

I had pretty well known who she was when I first approached her, but, you know, fun is fun. "Okay, I'll take that under advisement. But say, why don't you come with me? You don't want to be working all the time and these people seem to be getting along fine.

Nothing's going to happen to them that wasn't going to happen anyway. We could find another dance where you could have a better time."

"No, thank you. We're literally strangers, young man, and my responsibility is here. I *am* having a good time. You go and have yours somewhere else."

I couldn't resist saying, "At least come out to the car with me and have a beer." I knew she wouldn't agree to that, so I didn't have to worry about not having a car.

"I'll regard that as an improper suggestion. No thank you. Now I've told you what to do."

Dean Edith Rowles was a good sport, but she wasn't used to being hit on by ersatz students or pseudo-salesmen. She seemed to want to get higher on an indignant horse regarding my presence and actions, but on the other hand was somehow enjoying the situation. The dance number ended and I escorted her back to the divan. We conversed a few more moments, she reminded me that I was an interloper, we shook hands and I left for other parts of the large dance floor, as naturally I wasn't about to leave.

About three weeks later, I was playing tennis at the courts on the main campus, near the woman's residence where Dean Rowles had her office. A passing backhand cost me a point and the ball ended up against the chain-link fence behind the baseline, joining one sent there by a previously missed shot. After retrieving both balls, I straightened up and found myself gazing through the fence straight into the eyes of Edith Rowles.

"I see you're still at the university, Hal," she said. "Have you given up travelling salesmanship, or are you still an intruder?"

"Ah, as a matter of fact, well, yes. I'm taking classes."

"You're in Arts and Science, are you not?"

"You checked up on me! That's right. Now, about the other night..."

"You have a vivid imagination, Mr. Sisson, no need to explain."

"I enjoyed our dance. Perhaps we could do it again at some other function. And maybe you could recommend my dancing to some of the young ladies in your charge."

"Don't start up again. But drop in for tea some afternoon. I want to keep an eye on you."

"Thank you. Very kind of you. I'll do that."

"Goodbye." Dean Rowles left me standing there with my balls in my hand.

"Who's the old broad you were talking to, Hal?" my opponent asked. "Come on, let's get on with the game."

"She's not old, she's not a broad, she's the Dean of Women, so I'll thank you to treat her with some respect."

I got along well with Edith C. Rowles during the five years I was at the university. We had a few other dances together, but she never lined me up with a single date.

The Boozeborough

Hal Sisson

Saskatoon's Bessborough Hotel, aka the Boozeborough, was an imposing castle, an architectural legacy on the North Saskatchewan River. It was practically a de facto adjunct of the University of Saskatchewan campus. All the proms and balls were held at the hotel, where dolled-up co-eds paraded their youthful beauty before admiring stag lines who imagined them topless.

The Boozeborough's management was never as keen on university students as the students were on the hotel. Too much billingsgate, brouhaha, cachinnation and general hellery was the reason. It took a good deal of subterfuge for collegians to rent rooms at the hotel on dance nights. In the late forties, hotel detectives and desk clerks were trained to be the guardians of Christian behaviour and public morals. No matter that this was an anomaly, for the only place you could legally offer a person a drink was in your own home, or a hotel room where you were a registered guest. And the Woman's Christian Temperance Union would have outlawed that if they could.

I was part of a group of six or seven couples, all friends, attending a College of Commerce Ball just before Christmas one year. Bill Mahoney's girlfriend Marj had already graduated and lived in Regina, but returned to Saskatoon for this affair. At Bill's behest, we had her wire from Regina for a reservation, to thwart the Boozeborough ban on renting rooms to students.

Marj was actually staying with friends, so we had a female cohort check in during the afternoon under her name. The girl needed luggage to look legit. We bought a two-dollar suitcase from a second-hand store and packed the beer and Canadian Club rye into the case with lots of newspapers. Now we had a room on the fifth floor where we could all congregate and party in private while we came and went to the dance in the ballroom below. Bill stocked the room with mix and condiments after his classes were over for the day. In the process, he left some textbooks and class notes in the room, which he intended to pick up later. We were all to share in the costs.

The dance was swell, as they used to say. A good time was had by all, and out of deference to the hotel, we refrained from roasting marshmallows in the room. In fact, our behaviour was impeccable. The dance ended at midnight and the couples started drifting home. My girlfriend Charmaine and I out-waited everyone else until we were alone together in the room. As impecunious students, we didn't often get such an opportunity and were soon esconsed in bed. Natural earthly delights were just about to take place and breathing was getting heavy when the phone rang. Who in blue blazes could it be, we wondered. The room was registered in Marj's name and because the phone wouldn't stop ringing, Charmaine answered it.

"What is it?" she asked in a feigned sleepy voice, "I'm trying to get some sleep."

"This is the front desk, ma'am. You still have someone in your room. This is against hotel regulations and we'll have to ask all your unregistered guests to leave."

"What? I can't believe this! I'm here alone and trying to sleep! Good night!" She hung up.

"Good job," I said as I kissed her. "What business is it of theirs?" She kissed me back. I kissed her back. And we continued to kiss each other's back, sometimes switching to the front.

Ten minutes later the phone rang again.

Charmaine picked up the phone. A similar conversation ensued, with more vehemence on both sides, and she hung up again. We should have just refused to answer the phone. The door was locked, but we hadn't thrown the night lock or chain on the door. But who knew the dastardly depths to which the machiavellian minions of Canadian hotels would sink? How they could have made a profit with such an attitude is a mystery.

Not more than half a minute passed when we heard a key being inserted in the door. Kee-rist! Now what? we thought. Someone at the wrong door? No, the goddamn hotel dicks! They had a pass key!

In a classic reaction, repeated throughout the long march of history, I leaped naked out of bed and into the tall, spacious clothes closet common to all large railway hotels, the ones with the full-length mirror on the door. The bastard was checking the room. This was prime-time invasion of privacy, uncalled for and one would think illegal if you didn't know the Canada of that time.

I'll hand it to Charmaine, she protested vociferously in loud, abusive tones, ordering the man to leave her room, clutching the bedsheets to her breasts. The last place he looked was the clothes closet, but it was the only place for anyone to hide. The hotel dick started to open the door. I debated what to do. I would've liked to let him have a hard right to the chops, but that would mean even bigger trouble, so, standing there naked, I said, "Merry Christmas!"

There followed a sad, if not pathetic scene of frustrated passion and demands to know by what authority, etcetera. The night was ruined. We dressed. For some reason I picked up the two-dollar suitcase and the three of us proceeded in sullen silence down the hall to the elevator.

On the way down, the detective said, "One thing I can't figure out about your conduct."

"I can't figure out anything about yours, or the hotel's," I replied. "What is it?"

"Why'd you wish me a Merry Christmas?" he asked.

"Because you remind me of Scrooge!" I replied.

At the front desk the clerk demanded payment for the room. We were going to fix that up the next day, and I didn't have any money. Charmaine and I hadn't two dollars between us. I wouldn't have paid the Boozeborough if I'd been able, not after the kind of treatment they were dishing out. The clerk motioned for the dick to glom onto the suitcase, because he thought it was our luggage, and said they would hold it until the bill was paid.

"You're not holding that luggage," I cried out. "No, never, I want our belongings. You can't do that to us."

"Oh, yes we can," said both lackeys. An argument ensued in the lobby, with much shouting regarding the Hotel Act. They didn't have anyone's real name nor any other address for Marj except the city of Regina. There was nothing of value in the suitcase, so we put up a smoke screen fight over it, then resignedly let them have it and got the hell out of there.

Not dark and stormy, but it was one damnably cold December night and we had no money for a cab. It was late and there was little traffic for hitchhiking. We had winter coats for the long walk home, but even at that we nearly froze our butts crossing the windswept Twenty-fifth Street bridge to the other side of the river.

As far as I was concerned, the Boozeborough could kiss my ass for the rental. Mahoney was holding the money to pay, and I forget why it hadn't been done to start with.

But the story didn't end there, because of that damn suitcase. Mahoney's name was on the textbooks and class notes, which he'd placed inside the suitcase. The Bessborough manager contacted the university in the morning, and they passed on a message to Bill that the hotel would like to have a talk with him. Bill was mystified, but he went down there and was ushered into the manager's office.

"That was a pretty disgraceful exhibition you put on last night," said the manager.

I wasn't there so I don't know what all was said, but of course Mahoney denied that it was him. The upshot was that he paid the bill and figured out the score. He was mad! He caught me in the cafeteria that afternoon and gave me supreme hell. I tried to tell him it was the hotel's bloody fault. What right did they have to either invade someone's privacy or foist some cockamamie set of false public morals on fellow citizens and consenting adults who are minding their own business?

All Bill could see was that I'd besmirched the good name of his beloved bride-to-be and how could he possibly explain this fiasco to her? I couldn't figure out why she'd find out unless he told her. However, whether the hotel was in the right or not wasn't the point; I had been the one on the scene, the one responsible. Bill was a good friend and about all I could do was let him chew me out. If criticism hurt, skunks would be extinct. He didn't speak to me again for six weeks, although I tried to tell him that you should never feel compelled to stop a friend from getting laid; it was one of the perks of being a man.

Bill eventually got over it. He married Marj, they habbed livily ever after and the Christmas Commerce Ball at the Boozeborough occasionally came up to cause a round of laughter.

Huskie Football

Hal Sisson

It was the fall of fifty. There was no organized college football league in Western Canada at that time, only exhibition games with such junior teams as the Regina Rams and the Saskatoon Hilltops, and maybe the professional Roughriders from Regina. It was a pretty disorganized set-up with nothing at stake, except how badly we were going to be beaten. We liked to keep it close, like 45-9 or 52- 6. In the case of the Roughriders, it was more like 68-3.

Ted Preece, Doc Halliday, myself and someone else played the tackle positions in the line for the Huskies. In those days players played both offence and defence, you went both ways, stayed in for an indeterminate amount of time, and specialty teams had not been invented. You played in either the line, backfield or at end, unless you were the quarterback. I was the designated punter, and if I was playing tackle when the Huskies had to kick, which was more often than not, then one of the other tackles was sent in by the line coach. Simple system.

One long weekend, we played the Rams on Saturday and the Hilltops on the Monday holiday afternoon. For some reason in the Saturday afternoon game, the coach didn't play my best pal Ted Preece at all. We both thought this was eminently unfair, so with typical immature logic we proceeded to get drunk that evening in order to at least celebrate the loss.

Sometime during the festivities and revelry by night, I got the bright juvenile idea to phone Coach and remonstrate with him for not having played Ted in the game. Ted had practiced as hard as any of us and I figured he was a better football player than I was; my main talent was that I could kick the ball well. It was about one o'clock in the morning.

The coach answered and his voice indicated that he'd been awakened from his sleep. "Who is it?" I told him. "What do you want?"

"I want you to play my pal Ted Preece in the game on Monday. He didn't get to play today."

"Damn it, I'll decide that on Monday. And if I don't play him, it's nothing to you."

"If you don't play him, then we quit!"

"I know that's a threat, but I hope it's also a promise," Coach said before slamming down the phone.

We were hit with Sunday hangover, then Monday morning depression, but determination on both our parts not to let the side down (although maybe we would be doing so by showing up). We contritely went to the locker room early, well before game time. The coach was in his glassed-in cubicle. We knocked on the door, but he nearly didn't let us in.

"Now what?" he said resignedly.

"We've come to apologize for Saturday night."

"We were snapped up and we're sorry."

"What more can we say?"

"We just want to know if we should dress for the game or not."

Long pause. "You might as well," he said. "We're going to get a shit-kicking from this team, and it won't hurt my feelings if that extends to both of you personally."

We dressed, and Ted sat on the bench for the first quarter. The Hilltops were a young team, just under twenty-one most of them, big, fast and dedicated, destined to go places in junior football. They played hard, they played dirty, and they played to win. We weren't used to that approach. We were just a bunch of men having a final kick at the can in a team sport.

The second quarter was half over and the other two tackles were in the game when the coach looked down his bench and said, "Okay, Preece, your pal Hal wants you in the game. Get in there and show us what you can do. And I hope it's something big, because you all know the score."

Ted ran off the bench into the game and took his place at left tackle. On second down, the Hilltops ran an off-tackle line plunge by their fullback. His interference ran right over Preece and as he did so, he let him have a deliberately hard punch in the Adam's apple. Ted went down like he'd been axed. He was struggling and spluttering for breath. They had to carry him off the field in a stretcher and take him to the General Hospital in an ambulance.

He was still there the next evening when Ted's girlfriend Lois and I went to visit him. We'd brought a mickey in case he was in bad need of a drink. He wasn't. He lay in a private room. The desk nurse had said he'd be there for a couple of more days, and we were not to engage him in much conversation.

"How are you feeling, Ted?" we asked.

Ted motioned us to come closer to the bed and bend over, as he could only speak in a hoarse whisper, "Boy, Hal," he gasped, "you sure fixed me up good! With friends like you, I don't need any enemies!"

Only the Wryly-Witted and the Dim-Bulbed Need Apply

Dwayne Rowe

Anyone else out there tired of these entrepreneurial success stories that pop up regularly in the press? I don't begrudge any teenage computer expert a shot at becoming the next Bill Gates. But what about the ordinary adolescent geek who grows up to join what passes these days for adulthood, only to spend the rest of his life lurching from one financial fiasco to another? It's time some attention was paid to the members of this group.

There is, after all, a museum in the United States dedicated to supermarket items that never quite caught on. For instance, pre-mixed peanut butter and jelly in a jar. What wicked and capricious spirit of the marketplace decreed this wondrous invention to fail, while permitting the sale of Tang to flourish?

And if it weren't for Thomas Edison, we'd all be watching television by candlelight. Old Tom would work late into the night then finally pack it in, go home and proudly exclaim to his wife, "Erika (commonly misspelled as Eureka)! I have discovered ninety-eight ways how *not* to make a lightbulb!" Mrs. Edison would give forth with some sweet talk, tell him how brilliant he was (hence the derivation of Con Edison) and urge him to persevere, even though she would later confide to her friends that she thought his filament was stretched a little thin.

Then the fateful day arrived when Tom had manufactured a perfect bulb, but couldn't figure out a way to get it into the socket. His overworked brain suddenly snapped and in a fit of utter desperation, he grabbed his faithful assistant Herman Pinecone by the throat and hollered, "Screw it!" Herman did as he was told and the rest, as they say, is history.

It is Herman that I seek to honour, and all the other dim bulbs of the world, male and female, who, like Binky and Biff in the movies, are the leading lady's homely best friend, the sidekick to the hero or the third man through the door, who always gets killed. Also that pioneer rancher in the Cariboo region of BC, who hauled Alberta cattle over the Rockies in an old DC-3, flying solo, and went on to write his autobiography, *God is my Cow-Pilot*, only to have it cruelly rejected by some typically effete Eastern publisher.

The predictions of so-called psychics like Jeane Dixon are utter nonsense. The only person who accurately predicted the fall of the Berlin Wall was my Uncle Heinrich, who after thirty-five years of submitting bids, finally got a contract to repaint it.

My friend Harry and I were going through old issues of National Geographic (the equivalent of *Playboy* for any lad born in Saskatchewan before 1950) when we realized there were a lot of abandoned dugout canoes in South America. Apparently, with funding from the World Bank, everyone in the jungle got a new aluminum boat.

So we crafted a business plan and scooted down there courtesy of some frequently-scared-witless-and/or-bored-to-death bonus points and bought up every old canoe we could get our hands on. Next we air-freighted them back to BC, filled them in with Plastic Wood and rounded them off for logs, just in time to coincide with a downturn in the forest industry.

When our erstwhile friends and investors bug us for their money back, we hand them a financial statement from our cordial competitors Mac-Blo and Fletcher Challenge and huff, "Stop snivelling. Any investment is risky. Did we ever say we had a direct line to God?"

Undaunted, we found an acreage in Central Saanich, north of Victoria, and set up a roadside stand with this grabber of a billboard: *Factory-fresh eggs — zero grazing chickens — chemically enhanced vegetables.* Our market research consultant had assured us we were on the cusp of a monumental backlash against the granola-groping, yogurt-slurping, politically correct, self-righteous-twit consumerism so prevalent on the Island. Okay, so he was wrong. We lost a few bucks and our consultant is back doing opinion polls for people interested in opening neighbourhood pubs.

The point is that there's a certain beauty in having gone through experiences like that. It's like breaking your leg over and over again and each time, the new calcium growth heals the fracture and makes it stronger than ever (Warning: so far this is only theory). As a direct result, my buddy and I have gained the strength to proceed with our latest projects, which include a car compass that sticks to the dashboard with a magnet and safety belts for motorcycles.

Those of you who are sympathetic to the cause can help by reciting that venerable British Columbia good-luck incantation: Bella Bella, Bella Coola, Hugga Mugga, Boola Boola.

Mrs. Brown's Change and a Rest

Anon.

On March 17, 1915, there passed away Jane, beloved
wife of John Brown, aged thirty-one years. She leaves
a husband and several small children to mourn her
loss. Thy will be done.

"I don't know what I'll do," he said,
And a big tear splashed on his sunburnt hand,
"Here's spring upon us, my wife is dead,
And look at the summer's work I've planned!
I've bought more land, there are men to feed,
And hired girls are a careless breed,
They smash your dishes and waste your stuff,
And never think they're getting enough;
And they always boil the tea.
It wasn't like my Jane to quit—
She's always been so full of grit—
At least without saying a word to me."

"Then she wasn't ailing," the minister said.
He had come when he heard Mrs. Brown was dead,
to try and comfort the ones bereft.
"Oh! She grumbled as some women will
but she never cost me a doctor's bill.
Ain't this an awful way to be left.
She was a dandy, was my Jane,
strong as a horse and never complain.
I'll never get her like again.
Often when I had gone to bed,
she'd stay up and thump out loaves of bread.
And when I got up her work of the night
was there, a bunch of them brown and light,
I tell you, it was a splendid sight."

"I suppose you often told her so,"
the Minister said. "Well, I don't know,
I never was one to make a show.
But though I never said so straight,
I guess she knew I liked her gait."

"I suppose she had help," the Minister said,
as he looked at the work-worn hands of the dead.
"The house is large and children small,
One pair of hands could not do it all."
"We tried a girl for two or three days;
Jane was patient and thought she'd learn,
but she broke far more than she could earn.
Of course we always had Miss Frame
out here for a week when the children came.
And I tell you, I hated to pay for a week,
A dollar a day to that old freak.
The house was in one continual row,
Oh! I know well what I'm in for now."

"I suppose you always told your wife
that she was the joy and pride of your life;
that home wasn't home without her face
and how much you missed her from her place?"
"Well, maybe I didn't say so straight,
but I said things was in an awful state.
And I was tired of cold boiled tea
And Miss Frame couldn't quit too soon for me.
I told her my mother was never in bed
two days in her life, till she lay dead.
I've often and often heard that told—
she died when I was two days old."

"A splendid helpmate to you was given.
You have children, too?" "Yes, six or seven.
The youngest of them has not been strong,
we never knew just what was wrong.
See, here are the kids," and in two short rows,
Six children sat in their Sunday clothes.
Kind-faced women were busy there
Bestowing upon them unwonted care.
But the sad old wonder was in their eyes,
Which only comes when a mother dies.
The littlest one with the withered hand,
Nobody thought he could understand.
But he gathered up that air of gloom
And his voice rang out in that quiet room.
If ever a baby spoke despair
That little one cried, "It is not fair!"
"Come out a while," the father said,
"that kid's sharp voice goes through my head."
Outside was a day of sparkling sun
which wanes old winter, his days are done.
The cattle fine at the oat straw stacks

and fat pigs did long tunnelling stunts,
filling the air with contented grunts.
A young colt frolicked beside the mare
that lazily yawned in the soft spring air,
as she nosed it about with motherly care;
while hens and roosters cackled and crew
And openly gossiped of prospects, too.

"You have a lot of machines," the minister said,
looking around at the rakes and drills
which had overflowed from the big red shed.
"You've paid some big machinery bills."
Machines were there, blue, green and red,
a threshing machine with a canvas head;
while broken ones were weathered and grey
as if they had lain there many a day.
"We have to have them," said Mr. Brown,
"no matter what we have to pay.
The seasons are short and it's up to us
To make the most of every day.
These things cannot be borrowed or lent
So it's foolish to scrimp for the sake of a cent.
But of course a man must use his sense.
People try to do you every day.
It isn't more than a month ago,
a fellow came all around this way;
and he was surely a smooth-tongued gink
and was bound he would sell me a kitchen sink.
Jane would have taken it on the jump
for she's always wanted a kitchen pump.
But I showed her 'twould give us no return
and told her I hadn't no money to burn."

Then the neighbors came and they laid her away

And they blamed the Lord in the same old way,
And they wondered how if God is good
He could take her away from her hungry brood.
But looking down on that tired face
The minister knew what had taken place.
The Great Physician from the skies
Had looked on her with kindly eyes
And prescribed the cure he thought the best
For Mrs. Brown, "A Change and a Rest."
Then he did as the country doctors do
Not only wrote, but filled it too.
So the minister blushed as he read the words,
"Inasmuch as it hath pleased the Lord,"
And all the way home the grey bird's song
Piped out, "It's wrong, It's wrong, It's wrong."

Mrs. Brown passed out on St. Patrick's Day—
Mr. Brown dried his eyes by the end of May.
He painted his buckboards and looked abroad
And decided he'd try Bud Thompson's Maude.
For Maude was willing and big and strong
And he thought she'd be able to get along.
So he went to Maude and he laid his case
And told her he thought she'd a lovely face,
He'd always liked her quick, bright ways,
He believed he'd marry her some of these days.
Did she think she'd like to be his wife—
But Maude replied, "NOT ON YOUR LIFE!"

Neighbours

Anon.

"Who's that a-comin' up the path?
Run, Betsy Jane and see;
I'll bet its hateful old Miss Jones
A comin' here to tea!
Miss Perkins is it? Deary me!
I'd ruther hear it thunder;
She's allers out a-tattlin'.
What brings her here, I wonder?

I hope she's only come to call.
Don't ask her, dear, to stay,
For if you urged her long enough
She'd never go away.
Of all the wimmin that I know,
Miss Perkins beats them holler.
She's coming here to spy around,
I'll bet a silver dollar.
She's got her old silk bonnet on,

It's older than the hills!
I'm sure it looks ridiculous,
All ruffles, tucks and frills!
Good Gracious me, she's got her work—
I'll hev' to get my knittin';
I s'pose you knew Bill Smith had give
Her darter Ann the mitten.

Come in! Miss Perkins, is that you?
I'm desprit glad you've come;
For, as I said to Betsy Jane
The house seems awful dumb.
Miss Perkins, take the rockin' chair,
An' Betsy, take her bonnet;
Be sure you put it where the flies
An' dust won't get upon it.

Sez I, not half an hour ago,
Sez I to Betsy Jane,
I wonder where Miss Perkins is,
Why don't she come again?
Sez I, I hope she'll come today,
If nothin's up to hinder;
She's coming now, says Betsy Jane,
A-lookin' out the winder.

Miss Perkins, take a pinch of snuff,
An' tell us all the news,
I haven't heard 'em in so long
I've almost got the blues.
Miss Johnson got a new silk dress!
Miss Perkins, well, I never!
I wonder if she really thinks
Her money'll last forever!

Miss Perkins, yes, I was at church
Now wan't you glad to hear
The preacher preach so plain on dress?
It hit some folks so clear!
Miss Primrose colored, like a beet—
You know she wore a feather;
And Sarah Grimes was awful mad.
It hit them both together.

I wonder if Squire Pettibone
Hain't got a bran new wig?
I really do dislike that man
He feels so awful big!
You saw him walking t'other night,
Along with Katherine Snider?
Miss Perkins, that'll make a match,
I bet a pint of cider.

The deacon's son is waitin' on
Miss Grimes' cousin Rose—
I hardly know the reason on't,
What for, do you suppose?
I hardly think he'll marry her,
His father wont be willin',
For she's as poor as poor can be,
She isn't worth a shillin'!

I s'pose you know Marian Smith
Had named her darter Lily?
I'd call her Cabbage or Hollyhock—
That ain't a bit more silly.

Miss Perkins, have you heard about
That fuss with Pegleg Brown?

You hain't? Why goodness, gracious me,
It's all about the town.
They think he cheats his customers,
A-sellin' salaratus
An' say they've ketched his oldest son
A-stealin' green tomatoes.

Of course you've heard the talk that's round
About the widder Hatch;
They say she's after Thomas Sweet
And that'll be a match.
Her husband hain't been dead six months
And now she wants another;
She'd never be my da'ter-in-law
If I was Thomas' mother.

Have I heard of the weddin'? No!
Who underneath the sun?
John Wait and Huldy Robinson!
Miss Perkins, you're in fun—
Why, he's as much as fifty-two,
And Huldy isn't twenty.
But then you know the reason why—
The old fool's cash is plenty.

Miss Perkins, now twixt you and me,
My Betsy and your Anne
Are smart as any girls in town,
Deservin' of a man.
That spruce young cub in Talbot's store
As I was just remarkin',
Was here till ten last Sunday night—
I guess he thinks o' sparkin'.

Miss Perkins, are you going now?
One thing I'd like to know —
(Go bring her bonnet, Betsy Jane)—
What makes you hurry so?
Your bonnet's just as nice as new —
I swan! It's right in fashion;
Them ruffles an' them gathers there
Are really very dashin'.

Oh yes, Miss Perkins, I shall come,
You must come down ag'in;
You haven't been here in so long,
It really is a sin!
Good a'ternoon! Yes, Betsy Jane
Shall come an' see your da'ter.
There! Is she gone? I really hope
She got what she was a'ter!
In all my life I never did
See such a tattlin' critter,
They ought to call her "Scandal Bones" —
I'm sure the name would fit her.
I s'pose I must return the call,
For I wasn't sociable at all.

Advanced Parenting 303

Dwayne Rowe

In the event the title isn't sufficient warning, I want to make something very clear: the following material is not for that herd of gaga new parents, especially those yuppie types who waited until almost forty before breeding, in the hope that the genes responsible for bad choices and stupid behaviour would have been replaced by a DNA string believed to stimulate a passion for neurosurgery or highly leveraged hostile takeovers.

Further, it is definitely not designed for those mommy and daddy wannabes with ticking—or nowadays, liquid quartz crystal, digital readout—biological clocks counting off the fleeting days of dwindling fertility and fecundity.

Instead, it is a sharing of experiences with other battle-scarred combatants of the domestic wars, survivors of teenage rebellions, unwilling repositories of

unending angst emanating from their career-chal-
lenged and generally hopelessly addled children,
whose sole fixed purpose in life seemed to be avoid-
ing ever having to leave home. I hope this narrative
will recall some of the events occurring within your
own families and assuage whatever guilt you may
have been packing over the years.

I've always believed that if you want to look thin,
hang around with fat people. If at age sixty-one you
think you'd still enjoy being referred to as "that young
whippersnapper," then I suggest you move to
Camrose, Alberta or Sidney, British Columbia. In pur-
suance of this philosophy, I'm satisfied that upon considering the information I am about to disclose, you
will sit back, open a beer to go with the pizza and/or
that special box of wine you've been hoarding until
the last kid left home. After some purposeful reflec-
tion, followed by a moment of silence in memory of
the horrors you have endured as a parent, I am confi-
dent you'll be able to go on with a satisfied mind,
secure in the knowledge that by comparison, you
were a damn fine parent, after all.

My own childhood recollection of those groups
involving moms and dads and the smiley-faced
tyrants employed within the education system is that
they met sporadically and were known as home and
school associations. In my view—one shared by my
comrades—the purpose of that conspiratorial cabal
was that it called for you to get a licking at home for
the same reason you'd already got one at school.
Apart from tearing the arse out of one of the basic
tenets of our judicial system, the prohibition against
double jeopardy, it obliterated the concept of reasonable doubt, eradicated the right to make a full

defence before an impartial tribunal and seemed totally at odds with the fundamental principles of rehabilitation.

Fast forward to recent times. Imagine a prisoner on conditional parole, about to enter a halfway house. Rejoicing in the spirit of the Lord, dancing before the flames of freedom and embracing the concept he learned in the joint, that today is the first day of the rest of his life (watching Oprah is considered doing hard time), he buzzes for entry to his assigned rehabilitative facility. The administrator, knowing the nature of the crime committed and the extent of the punishment previously imposed, greets him at the door and promptly punches him in the kisser. I'm not a criminologist by trade, but I suspect there's a flaw in the program.

By the time my wife and I were raising our own kids, the interactive mechanism utilized to bring into collision the raging egos of elementary school teachers and the shell-shocked, perennially exhausted parents was now known by some variant of parent-teacher association, a term adopted from our American neighbours.

Roseanne and I had married, each for the second time, in a triumph of hope over experience. Each brought two children to the chaotic dinner table, so we had one boy, aged ten, and three girls, nine, eight and seven respectively. If you do the math, by adding four years, then you can appreciate that one pubescent, hormone-twisted she-devil emerged from a previously lovable larvae state each year for three consecutive years, and each alternated between a funk and a fugue state for another six. I remember hollering to my wife: "I can't stand any more of these funk 'n fugues!" In attempting further description, words fail me—something to do with the combined effects of accumulating bile and rising gorge—but think of the flip side of the Brady Bunch, a troop of aliens from a parallel universe temporarily unable to return to their pod and instead, living in your house.

When the kids starting bringing home various notes from their teachers, I would respond by writing a reply using a thick carpenter's pencil and scraps of paper, preferably brown, ripped from shopping bags. I would then fold the paper, mostly by crumpling it, seal it with a sliver of shiny duct tape, label it for the attention of the particular educator involved and hand it to the relevant child for return to sender. If for example, the teacher had notified us that Denise required a new lunch box and thermos in order to appropriately transport her noon-time meal, then I replied as follows:

Dir Teech:

It jist seem like yisterday I bot her one butt she probly done busticated it real good. Tho' we is pore folk, I will kill a hog and git enuff to buy one latter this week.

Denise's Pa

I was not letting my wife Roseanne in on this scam, but merely informed her that Denise needed a new lunch kit.

A week or so later, Debbie came home with a note requesting that we inform the school authorities whether we had any concerns about her going on a field trip. If we had no objections, we were to sign a waiver, to be placed on file with the school board's weasel insurance company. I wrote a note in which I stated unequivocally:

Dir Miz Ellie:

Bout that trip. I ain't one for gallyvantin sted of gittin booklarnin, but I done talked to the Missus and I guess it don't make us no nevermind.

Debbie's Pa and Ma

Over the course of several months I probably sent a dozen notes in the same vein. I once wrote a note to excuse Michele from missing a day at school. I explained it was "cuz she cotched some kind of flu and woz swetting like a dog lying up agin an airtite stove." When Allan received a high mark on a math test, his teacher sent a genuinely congratulatory note because he had told her we insisted on his completing his homework. I wrote back:

Dir Teechur:
Thankee kindly for them praiseful words. His Momma and me is prouder 'n pigs.

One time, Roseanne, having forsaken wearing any of her fifty-four pairs of shoes, managed to sneak up on me (I always meant to buy a little necklace-bell) and caught me writing one of my homespun epistles. She read it over and I heard that click which means—if you have XY chromosomes—you've got thirty-five seconds to climb into your suit of armour

before the white heat of female XX fury comes blast-
ing your way. I attended a Robert Bly seminar once,
and his theory is that if a man misses that warning
sign and fails to get properly prepared, he will
become the object of an unleashing of a thousand
years of anger and resentment on behalf of millions of
women, long dead, as channeled through their chosen
living representative now screaming directly into his
face. I must have been relying on basic survival skills
back then but even so, I barely made it. I was, however,
smart enough to blurt out a sincere promise to stop
fooling around with any aspect pertaining to school
and/or the kids' education. And I did, mainly because
no more messages arrived that needed my specialized
attention.

I forgot about the whole episode and one evening
went along with Roseanne to a parent-teacher interview. It's called that, but it's actually a teacher-to-par-
ent lecture. We sat down in those crappy little midget
chairs in front of a huge desk where the lovely, mini-
skirted, twenty-eight-year-old Miss Whatever was
seated. We identified ourselves as Debbie's parents.
Roseanne, as usual, looked like she'd just finished a
fashion shoot for *Vogue*. As for moi, comme d'habi-
tude, as we say in Girouxville, Alberta, I was wearing
jeans, plaid shirt, baseball cap and cowboy boots.

The teacher greeted Roseanne effusively, and they
had a little chat about Debbie's amazing improvement
in her reading skills and what a cheery, tiny, precious
child she was and such a pleasure to have in the classroom, blah-blah-blah. Then the teacher turned and
staring right at me, enunciated very clearly and slowly, "And...how...are...you...tonight?"

"Pretty good," I replied, thinking maybe a piece of

my tattered ball cap had come loose and was hanging down around my ear so she figured I was wearing a hearing aid. Then she leaned across her desk and with astounding clarity and diction, she asked, "What...kind...of...work...do...you...do?"

It came to me in a blaze—just as the snake-eye-removing portion of Roseanne's high-heeled pump got me in the lower calf just where the boot top ends—and I thought, Those damn notes, they've come back to bite me on the ass! It seemed like an hour but it was probably only a few seconds. I sat up very straight and leaned forward on the desk so my nose and that of the gorgeous teacher lady were about two inches apart and I told her very precisely, "I...am...a...law...yer."

She panicked and starting rummaging around, frantically reviewing her prepared interview material, then reached inside her drawer and brought out some of the notes I had written, from what must have been Debbie's student file. She looked at Roseanne, desperate for some explanation.

Roseanne illuminated the room with her hundred-thousand-kilowatt smile, whispered something to her in confirmation of my bizarre revelation and added, "He's feeling much better now." They both nodded in that way women have when consigning men to a special cave within the Valley of Idiots, and even though the teacher probably still figured I was dumber than a sack of hammers, at that moment I sure as hell was smart enough to know the interview was over and I would be watching TV downstairs—profoundly alone – well into the night.

Although I recovered from the phony-note incident, I found myself in trouble again as a result of saying to one of the kids, who wanted a new something-or-other, that we didn't have the money right then and were, in fact, poor. A week or so later, Debbie came home with a new notebook, crayons, pencil, binder and sundry supplies. Roseanne inquired how she had come into such a windfall and Debbie related that she had simply told the teacher that her family was really poor and so her teacher had taken up a collection among her colleagues to purchase supplies for such a sweet, tiny, precious treasure, blah-blah-blah.

Roseanne went to speak with the homeroom teacher (I was not invited) and made a generous donation to square things which, apart from being grandiose and totally unnecessary, failed to gain any ground in our ongoing domestic war against poverty.

Another time, Debbie was complaining about doing some homework and I told her, "Quit school. I can get you a job in the cornflakes factory." She was in grade five at the time, and the next day my wife received a call from the principal requesting that she attend at the school—immediately—to discuss a serious matter.

Apparently, the same teacher had discovered Debbie in the act of packing all of her new supplies and other personal items into a pillowcase she had brought from home. When questioned about her intentions, Debbie informed the teacher we were still poor—despite what her Mother had said—and she was going to take the job her Dad had lined up for her at the cornflakes plant. That evening, I dug myself out of that hole by being honest and open with her about matters concerning her career. I told her, flat out with no sugar coating, that the Kellogg people had decided not to open up shop in Edmonton but would be staying in London, Ontario. I took out the road atlas and showed her where that was and she agreed with me that it would be a bitch of a commute.

With the passing years, one could see Debbie's gullibility level recede to the point where there was barely a trace of what had once existed. After many years of studying and working, she obtained her designation as a Certified Management Accountant. Later, during employment in an auditing position, she would stare directly at some poor bugger on the hot seat clutching his virtual sack of truly bogus business expenses and, eschewing the usual reference to falling off the back of the proverbial turnip truck would, in that icy, neutral, Hannibal Lecter voice common among auditors, issue this unambiguous declaration: "Listen, Mister, I didn't just come out of a cornflakes factory."

All of our kids were born before the advent of the national medicare system. In those days in Alberta, the doctors operated their own medical scheme called MSI, which was an abbreviation for Medical Services Inc. Depending on the number of individuals covered, there was a monthly premium and the provincial government had created a subsidy program for low-income earners. For the typical healthcare consumer, there were no extra charges throughout the entire period of pregnancy or for post-partum office visits, provided you were satisfied with the services of an ordinary general practitioner.

However, if you wanted a fancy obstetrician to deliver the baby, there was a supplemental charge, in the same sense that one now has to pay extra for real Kalamata olives or anchovies in most pizza joints. The doctors operated the entire program themselves, including the complicated process of premium billing and issuing payments to physicians in accordance with an established scale. When the architects of the Just Society ordered this entirely workable program to be abandoned for the greater good, the doctors offered to transfer to the federal government, free of charge, their entire computerized accounting network and administrative base.

Sensing a trick, the Ottawa bureaucrats decided instead to seek out their own distinguished panel of experts, including a retired allergist and a dermatologist, and in a rash decision, opted to rely on their advice to start over from scratch. As a result of being from northern Alberta and growing up with a fierce sense of independence, when the radio stations played that saccharine theme song from the movie *Born Free*, it would make me upchuck. I think the doctor—or maybe it was the priest—said it had something to do with ad nauseum, which until then I thought was caused by continual exposure to those decibel-enhanced commercials by The Brick. Born Free!? In a pig's eye, my friends. Michele cost me an extra ninety bucks for the specialist. The fact that he forgot to show up, and that an intern or orderly or someone called Big Jimmy, who had been called in to refill the Pepsi machine, arrived in the delivery room just in time to catch her, did not entitle me to one penny in refund.

Knowing that sooner or later this new system was going to suffer a shortfall, my wife and I hit upon a surefire method to tell whether one of the kids was actually sick or just faking it in order to skip school. We would send in our little dog, Muffet, remembered as the Poodle from Hell. Muffet once chewed the backs out of twelve of Roseanne's fifty-four pairs of shoes. She also sucked all the juice out of a case of Kiwanis apples, leaving them so light they nearly floated away. We used to board her at kennels and always received free accommodation if we promised the operators she would never return to arouse the entire caged population every night.

Muffet may have had her idiosyncrasies, but she was a brilliant diagnostician. We nicknamed her Dr. Snuffalopagous because she would leap onto the bed, sniff and lick various parts of the purportedly ill youngster, wiggle her way under the covers, snuggle up against the child and then pronounce the verdict. If she snorted derisively and leaped off the bed to run downstairs and torment Jody, our other dog, then the kid was faking and the appropriate punishment for incompetent con artists was meted out—after school.

Denise had extremely white skin and one could see the bluish capillaries barely under the surface, so she was a tough nut to crack because she could look really sick almost at will. However, if we let Muffet into the bedroom for a quick consultation and the good Doctor remained curled on the bed next to that fragile, tiny body—usually curved ito a pitiful fetal position—then we knew the kid really was sick and we would let her stay home for the day.

Camping proved to be the best family activity we ever shared. In the 1975 season, we spent at least forty nights in the tent trailer, sleeping along lakes, streams and rivers, and it was a joyful experience. Everyone mastered a series of tasks and we could set up camp in an hour and break it down in less than that, with every-thing in its assigned place. All the kids could clean a pan-sized rainbow trout in a few seconds. My wife always ran a well-ordered home and she imported her

talents to the campground. We'd complete each season's shakedown trip and make a list of additional
items we required and from then on, we had everything imaginable, including a fold-up wire picket
fence and a patch of green outdoor carpet. We packed
a canoe on the roof of the car and fished from dawn to
sunset, which at Two Lakes in the mountains near
Grande Prairie doesn't arrive until eleven p.m. and
even then it's not really dark. The rainbow trout
seemed to want to commit suicide and impaled their
delicious little bodies on our flies and spinners.

We visited places like Moonshine Lake, Bird's
Pond, One Island Lake and Saskatoon Lake, and
travelled down the Wapiti and Smoky Rivers. One
time at Moonshine Lake, Allan and I were fishing out
of the canoe, trolling flies, as we paddled slowly
about fifty feet out from the bank. The proximity of
land must have triggered a response, because he told
me we had to pull in to shore so he could pee. A couple of J-strokes later, we angled up to the grassy bank
and he jumped out of the bow and began tearing
down a narrow, willow-lined footpath bordering the
lake, heading for an outdoor biffy in a clearing about
a hundred feet away.

The trail followed the edge of the lake in a direct
line for fifty yards and then because the shoreline jut-
ted in a bit, it abruptly bulged to the right like the cul-
de-sac on the small intestine caused by an appendix,
after which it ran dead true once again for another
hundred yards past the open patch housing the toilet.
The chasm between the straight portions—created by
the sudden loop on the trail—was only about fifteen
feet wide.

The only thing I can figure is that at the speed

Allan was travelling, he must have been looking down
when he arrived at the section of the path that suddenly veered right. With his thirteen-year-old legs
pumping away like pistons, he just kept on running,
right off the trail and into the lake. It was like one of
those cartoons where the coyote realizes he's gone
over the cliff. For a moment, gravity is suspended,
then with a look of puzzlement, down he goes.

Allan was wearing one of those cloth caps with a
tiny round fabric-covered button on top. That was the
first thing I noticed. His cap floated to the surface and
a puff of afternoon breeze pushed it away from shore.
He came up splashing, sputtering, dog-paddling,
frantically trying to get his bearings, desperately trying to understand what in hell had happened to him.
He spotted me sitting in the stern of the canoe.

I was absolutely paralyzed with laughter. The
sight of his little sunburned forehead poking above
the surface and his cap bobbing about just beyond his
reach was too much for me. I couldn't do anything to
help Allan, who was a good swimmer despite his
instinctively reverting to the dog-paddle, except to
repeat, "I'm sorry, I'm really sorry," and then roll over
again on the thwarts, holding my aching gut.

At some point, I remember him arriving at the
canoe, jumping into his assigned position as bow-
man, angrily shoving off, ducking his head while
paddling away, using slashing, rapid strokes to propel
us in the direction of camp.

I managed to settle down for a few seconds, except
when we slowed down just enough for Allan to use
the fishing net to recover his half-submerged cap. A
wicked vision of the poor little bugger out for an afternoon stroll—along the lake bottom—broke me up all

over again and I could barely help paddle any longer, except for the odd stroke to keep the canoe on course.

Back at camp, Allan told his mom about the episode, which was bad enough, but also our friend Jim Stearns, the senior probation officer. In his confusion, the poor kid obviously thought Jim had the power to apprehend children from neglectful parents, but as the nice lady at the 1-800 Children's Help Line later informed him, that authority was exercised by another government department.

Drying out around the campfire, wringing out his cap, Allan told me, "You know, I forgot to go pee."

"That's okay, son," I said. "I went for you. Remind me to bail out the canoe."

The children learned other things from me in the world of sports, leisure and plain fun. On a really windy day, Allan and I liberated new bedsheets, still in their store packaging, to improvise sails to pull us around on our bikes. There was a new subdivision in Grande Prairie with streets and sidewalks, except there were no houses on the lots yet. Allan sat on the handlebars, where we tied one end of the sheet and he held another corner of the material. I was in the captain's seat, steering with one hand and desperately clinging to another tail of the sheet to provide a full spinnaker effect.

We tacked back and forth on a quartering reach until the following wind suddenly died off to nothing. The bike was travelling at a pretty good clip at that point, and our sail collapsed and became entangled in the spokes, with the immediate effect of halting our forward movement and sending Allan flying off the handlebars onto a mound of dirt adjacent to a virgin sidewalk. A police car happened to pass by with

Dolores Beacon, another probation officer, in the passenger seat. When the RCMP officer asked her who the idiot was on the bike, she told him it was the rookie Criminal, Family and Juvenile Court provincial court judge.

We lived in Medicine Hat for two summers. Rudyard Kipling said about that place: "It has all hell for a basement." He was apparently referring to the abundant supply of subterranean natural gas, but it truly is hotter there than Hades in August. I love to record the weather, and in the summer of 1977, the average daily high was about thirty-two degrees Celsius.

I insisted the kids get out every day and not just spend all their time in our root-cellar-like basement family room or at the neighbourhood outdoor pool. One day when it was about thirty-eight degrees, I got them playing baseball and they were chasing fly balls and running after my spectacular line drives. I impressed upon the girls that it was critical for them not to look like girls when they were running or throwing a ball, and they worked on honing those skills. We dealt with other fundamentals and techniques needed to participate in one of the best games ever devised. After all, hockey is played on a rink and football on a field, but baseball is played on a diamond.

Later that night, at the emergency ward, a non-judgmental apple-cheeked intern took a few minutes from her busy rounds to lecture us as a family on the importance of maintaining adequate electrolyte levels. The girls have never forgotten that special event, and if it sometimes slips from my memory, one of them will do whatever it takes to restore it. It's their version of *Je me souviens*.

Just before being advised that my transfer from Grande Prairie to Medicine Hat had been approved by the chief judge, we had shipped Michele off to summer camp for four weeks. When word came through about our move, we did the usual things like selling the house and packing up all our stuff, and with Roseanne driving one car and me following in the other, we headed off to The Hat.

To this day, I am positive I had taken a moment out of my busy schedule to ask the camp administrator to tell Michele that we were no longer living in Grande Prairie. I accept that I may have neglected to provide exact details of our temporary accommodations along our travel route, but I'm willing to take a polygraph that I clearly spelled out we were heading for the southeastern corner of Alberta. Once you narrow it down to that region and you eliminate Seven Persons and Bow Island, the Hat is the obvious destination.

To make things worse, I had forgotten to mark down the last day of camp, so she had to hitch a ride with someone going through to Moose Jaw who was kind enough to drop her off. Today, Michele is the mother of four children and a proud graduate of the University of Regina with a degree in social work, and as one would expect, has a varied caseload dealing with the special emotional needs of both children and adults. When we get together, we rarely discuss specific details of our respective professions, but it seems to me that she devotes a disproportionate amount of time to dealing with Generation X-ers still struggling with abandonment issues.

It's clear that though we may stumble around sometimes in an impenetrable fog or bobble the ball on occasion, we still try to do our best with our children and grandkids. Back then, children didn't arrive with an instruction manual, except for that Dr. Spock guy. But who wants to take advice from some pointy-eared space freak? The kids turned out just fine and they are decent, hard-working citizens, thanks for the most part to the unending efforts of my wife, who cooked, cleaned, clothed and globally cared for them, and to me, sometimes around the clock if illness paid a visit to our home.

Apart from the updates I have already provided on Debbie and Michele, in order to round out this tale, I can tell you this: Denise continues to despise miniature poodles, but she can proofread at fifty paces, and when she sends a three-page e-mail, you'd be damn lucky to find even one piddly spelling or grammatical error. Allan enjoys designing websites and gardening, but still refuses to go swimming fully clothed. Depending on whether it's summer or the rainy season, he risks incurring either sunstroke or dry rot because he is perpetually bare-headed. He hates all kinds of hats, especially those cloth caps with the tiny, round button on top.

A Son of the Beach

Hal Sisson

I'm Tony Peroni, a sonna da beach,
I live on da lakeshore where da seagull she screech,
I'm not like my brudda, for him and I each,
Are two deeferent kinds of sonna da beach...

Old-timers' disease may have robbed me of my ability to remember the rest of that poem, which in any case would now be considered politically incorrect, even though I have no intention of maligning either Italians or my brother. However, I can still recall how the summer holidays of my youth were spent. Lord knows, teachers asked us to write enough English essays on the subject, which was a bind and a chore. We didn't have the moxy to tell the truth about those too-recent life experiences, which are all history now. The main trouble with history is that almost every day is the anniversary of something awful.

Way back when, sometime or other during the summer, everyone went to a beach. It made no matter what the real name of the place was, they just said they were going to *The Beach,* one of a hundred or more across the western prairies, blessed havens from the oppressive heat of city and farm. You could swim or boat all day long, not just in a muddy slough or pond, but in a real lake with sandy beaches. You made summer friends at a beach, different from the ones you had at home and school, and for a while you lived a different life.

I grew up in Moose Jaw, Saskatchewan, which, as my Uncle Murray used to say, was the crossroads of the world, where the highways and the byways met at the gateway to the western world, an ideal manufacturing centre; and there was a women's lavatory in city hall. Later on they even built a comfort station on Main Street.

School in Moose Jaw ended the last week in June. Our family was at the beach by July first and stayed till Labour Day in a ramshackle old cottage named Braeside, purchased by my widowed mother from an elderly friend, Ma Martin, for a hundred dollars (ten down and ten a year). The price sounds ridiculous now, but that was back in the early thirties. My mater only got there for a two-week holiday, as she worked in the hot heart of the dust-bowl city.

My grandmother was the babysitter for the four children. This grand old dame always assiduously prepared for the summer sojourn by making an advance supply of foodstuffs. The one I remember best bore the strange name of rissoles. This was a fast food before its time: precooked meat patties stored in large mason jars filled with the lard from their own

cooking process. All they needed was re-heating and a
supply of buns and you had instant hamburgers.
Today, since no one depends on the ice wagon, and
everyone owns a refrigerator, rissoles are redundant.

Lumsden Beach was on Last Mountain, also
known as Long Lake, in southern Saskatchewan. The
lake *was* long, but where the name Last Mountain
came from I've never understood, for there isn't a
mountain within five hundred miles. You can't begin
to see the Rockies from there. Wishful thinking, I suppose, on the part of Western pioneers. The beach
exerted a strong geographical pull on my heartstrings,
forming a good part of the emotional map of my
youth. I spent every July and August there from 1930
to 1939, from age nine to nineteen.

We would head out the old Moose Jaw-Regina
highway in my Uncle Tom's Terraplane, through the
sometimes harsh and desolate drought-racked land-
scape. Then we'd cut north at Pence and come into the
Qu'Appelle Valley southwest of the prairie oasis river
town of Lumsden.

Beyond the town, we'd drive up the steep escarp-
ment on the other side, where, on the sloping face of a
big hill, there was always a large white sign in jumbo
letters carved into the face of the hill for all travellers
to read. It was intended to urge everyone to *EAT
FRED'S BREAD*, but some jokers were continually
rearranging the lettering to read *BEAT (or EAT)
FRED'S HEAD*, or *FRED'S BAD BREAD*, or *HEAT
FRED'S BED*. Local wiseacres getting their kicks, a
standing joke in Lumsden Town. The materials for the
sign were planks painted white, or perhaps white-
washed rocks, or sacks of cement. I never went up the
hill to find out. Whoever Fred was, he must have had

one helluva time climbing up and down that hill to correct his sign. I'm sure it gave him an unusual slant on life.

The sign inspired similar efforts on my part, as witness the following excerpt from the Moose Jaw *Times-Herald* newspaper of the time: "Evidence of a humourist at work can be seen on No. 1 Highway leading East from Moose Jaw to Regina. Just at the outskirts of Moose Jaw the government erected a road sign reading *SLOW, WATCH FOR BREAKS IN PAVE-MENT*. Someone, who had apparently just made the trip from Regina to Moose Jaw over what is supposed to be a hard surface road, but resembles instead a stretch of ground recently subjected to heavy bombing, spotted the sign and made some changes. It now reads: *SLOW, WATCH FOR PAVEMENT!*"

Lumsden Beach was religion-oriented, dominated by WASPs of right-wing persuasion: Methodists, Wesleyans and Presbyterians who had recently formed the United Church of Canada. They were among the reasons I didn't grow up to be a fan of organized religion of any denomination. Unlike chicken soup, religion may not help, but it can hurt you. On Sundays you weren't allowed to swim on the wide, sandy, main beach with its raft and slide. The powers that be, the beach elders, even padlocked the swings. The result wasn't quite what they'd had in mind, for this attitude only taught some of us to fight bureaucratic authority wherever it was found.

Sunday Beach

Hal Sisson

On Sundays the weak of faith, the iconoclasts, the hot and the sweaty traipsed half a mile north up the lake to Sunday Beach, where we swam from a narrow boulder-strewn bit of foreshore. Strangely enough, this swimming spot was situated just below a property owned by a summer camping organization that rented out the facilities each year—a complex of bunkhouses and a mess hall—to various religious groups throughout the season. Luckily, they often catered to girl's camps, which in theory increased our possible number of contacts with defecting females. Who knew, one of them might even expose her pop tarts on the beach.

Cars were hard come by in the late thirties, certainly by those of high-school age. Only one guy I knew, Bryce Rollins, big brother to Al Rollins of NHL goalie fame, whose father owned a garage on Manitoba Street, had regular use of a car. Bryce snaffled a loaner from his dad for two weeks. He and I, along with Norm and Mel Pratt, rented our own cottage at the beach, as befitting grade twelve students. Our problem soon became that of ready cash. After paying the rent we had sufficient money for gas, plus enough to get to Regina Beach regularly, with enough pocket money for admission to the two dance halls in that southern Saskatchewan mecca, the Ark, a made-over lake boat, and the Terrace, just across the railway tracks. Also a necessity were Cokes, chips and ice cream for dance partners or dates.

"Where can we get some food?" I asked the question on all our minds. After all, we had to eat every day.

"I've been thinking about that," replied Norm. "There's the girls' camp down at Sunday Beach, the Canadian Girls in Training."

"What are they in training for?" asked Bryce. He got the standard salacious replies.

"Look," said Norm, "they set up the mess hall every night in preparation for an early breakfast. They put out loaves of bread—"

"What, no fishes?" his older brother Mel interrupted.

"Shut up and listen! And pounds of butter and pails of jam on the tables. They don't even lock the screen doors. I've seen it."

"So?" we all asked.

"So we hit the mess hall tonight when we get back from the dance at Regina Beach," said Norm, who was later to join the Royal Canadian Mounted Police.

"Are you kidding? The last time I checked, that was called stealing," I protested.

"No," said Norm, "it says right in the Bible, in John 21: 9-15: 'As soon then as they were come to land, they saw a fire of coals there, and fish laid thereon, and

bread...and Jesus saith unto them, "Come and dine." '
Now is that not an invitation to partake of bread laid
out before us?"

Norm Pratt wasn't a minister's son for nothing.
He'd had to listen to a lot of Bible quotes in his time.

"You mean they have fish there, too?" said Bryce.

"It's not a fish camp, it's a girl's camp, and they only
lay out bread and condiments. There are fish in the
lake. We can go fishing if you want fish," Norm said.

"Is he right about that quote from the Bible?" I
asked.

Mel replied, "Yeah, he's right. And he should also
have quoted Obadiah, First Kings, 18: 24: 'For it was
so, when Jezebel cut off the prophets of the Lord, that
Obadiah took an hundred prophets and fed them in a
cave with bread and water.' Maybe that's what the
Good Lord intended those virgins down at the camp
to do—provide bread and sustenance to hungry way-
farers in the night."

Mel was not to be outdone by his younger brother,
and what impressed me the most, he must actually
have been listening when his father preached.
Personally I thought they were faking the chapter and
verse; anybody can make up numbers.

"Sounds reasonable to me," Bryce chimed in. "We
wouldn't want to go against the word of the Lord or
seem ungrateful for bounty which is literally being
thrust under our very noses by the Fates."

I like to think that I was dating the lady counsellor
out at the CGIT camp at the time. She was older than
I and likely merely indulging my youthful fancies, as
there was little big game for her to hunt in the area.
She used to sneak away from her charges after lights
out to go to dances at Regina Beach with us. I really

didn't want her to know about this plan. That was my main objection to the proposed bread, butter and jam heist, but we were in a dilemma and I liked the rationalizations promulgated by the Pratts. I also liked the sin of dancing too much to raise any objections. The camp might have given us the staff of life and the condiments to place on it if we had asked them, but our pride wouldn't let us beg. We'd rather steal. No high moral ground captured here by our testosterone-driven decision.

Bryce was an expert driver. He came as fast as he could manage up the last rise in the road before we hit the camp, cut the lights and killed the engine. He put her into neutral and let the car coast down the slight incline, then up the other side of the dip right up to the mess hall, and with a ninety-degree turn and stop, ended up facing the way he'd come.

No door slamming. In our stocking feet, the Pratts and I checked the screen door. It wasn't latched, so there was no breaking here, only entering. Norm began throwing pails of jam and pounds of butter into a gunny sack, while Mel and I grabbed as many loaves of bread as we could pile up in our arms, and we all headed back out the door. No fish; this wasn't Galilee and we weren't about to throw our bread upon the waters of Long Lake.

Everything was dumped into the back seat, Bryce put the car into neutral gear and let it coast back down into the dip in the hills. As we reached the bottom, he turned on the ignition and slowly and quietly headed back down the road toward Lumsden Beach. A good getaway man. Over the first low wooded hill we stopped and walked back to take a look. Not a light, not a sound from the Camp.

"It is more blessed to give than to receive," said Norm, "and may the Canadian Girls in Training inherit the Kingdom of Heaven."

"You and Mel sure as hell won't," said Rollins. "It's okay for Sisson and I to do this, because we don't know that it's wrong the way you two do, being, as it were, the sons of Abraham. I'm ashamed to associate myself with your ilk."

"Shut up and drive us out of here," said both Pratts. "We're hungry."

When we laid out our haul at the cottage, the jam was all strawberry and I hate strawberry. "For God's sake, Norm, why couldn't you look for some orange marmalade?" I asked.

"You couldn't tell in the dark," he replied. "Maybe there wasn't any. Why didn't you get some cracked wheat? This bread's all white."

"Who's going to say grace?" asked Mel.

"I will," said Bryce. "'The floor of the death cell he paced, he must pay the wages of sin. The warden said, "You have one hour of Grace." He said, "Okay, send her in!"'"

We lived on bread, butter and strawberry jam and drank tap water; that was our punishment and after a week we felt that we'd paid our debt to society.

The Tin Temple

Hal Sisson

In the mid-thirties, the traditionalist Christian group the Oxford Movement was popular among the youth of Saskatchewan. The Movement conducted a summer camp at Lumsden Beach, long noted for its religious zeal and the observance of the Lord's Day Act. Sunday school classes were held in a building on pilings in a wooded hollow in the village. The Tin Temple, as the place was known, boasted a corrugated metal roof, a plank floor and screen windows on three sides.

As a lad I was quite often near that edifice along with the evil companions into whose company I had fallen. They shall remain nameless to protect the guilty.

One of the bad influences on me at the time (or was it I on him?) was Mel Pratt, the son of the Rev. J.W. Pratt, the minister to the Zion United Church in Moose Jaw.

How near did Mel and I get to the meetings of the

Oxford Movement in the Tin Temple? From the slope above the well-treed hollow, you could glimpse parts of the tin roof glinting in the sun. From that vantage point one day, we rained handfuls of small pebbles and fair-sized rocks down on the roof. This made an ungodly racket inside the temple.

We unloaded all our ammo, then headed for the hills like big-assed birds, as the young disciples of the Oxford Movement poured out of the hall like angry wasps searching for their tormentor. We were never caught in the act but were under heavy suspicion for loitering with intent.

One day the following week, the sun was smiling down on the beach, as it always did, and the wind was blowing up some small whitecaps on Long Lake. Three of the Oxford lads approached Mel and I in a friendly manner and asked if we'd like to come for a ride in their sailboat. It was the sort of offer boys don't like to refuse.

We sailed out into the middle of the lake. Great sport, good clean fun. Opposite the Sea Scout Camp on the other side, they hove to and dropped both the sail and the anchor. Then they turned toward Mel and I.

"Would you like to tell us about throwing rocks at the Tin Temple?" asked one of the six-foot-tall, hundred-and-eighty-pound disciples of the Golden Rule.

"Would you care to rephrase that question?" replied Mel, feigning as much innocence as he could muster on short notice.

"Yeah, what are you talking about?" I chimed in, probably too quickly and too nervously.

"You two know what we mean," said another member of the lynching party. "And you want to confess,

don't you? In fact, we insist that you confess." With
that, two of them grabbed us in headlocks.

"What would it take to convince you that we're
innocent?" I asked through my narrowing windpipe.
The guy was strangling me.

"Nothing. We know you did it," said the leader
helmsman. "We just want your confession—an act of
contrition on your part and promises not to repeat
your sins."

"I didn't know you guys were Catholic," Mel
replied.

"You smartasses, you're going overboard if you
don't come clean!" With that, the goon squad thrust
our heads and shoulders over the gunwales.

"Can you swim that far?" I whispered to Mel as
our heads pressed together and touched the water.

"They're bullshitting," he whispered back.

"Don't count on it. They could be some of those
religious fanatics you read about."

"Well, what's it going to be, kiddies?" shouted the
captain. "Are you going to smarten up or what?"

They dunked our heads underwater. As we came
up we started to yell. "You got us all wrong!" "You
have no proof—we're innocent!" "We want a fair
trial!" "Your Mothers wear army boots!" "I'd understand you better if my I.Q. were lower."

But our protestations died beneath the surface of
the lake as we went overboard into the drink.

As we struggled toward shore through the waves,
in and out of patches of thick seaweed, I asked,
"Would they have the guts to let us drown?" I figured
Mel, with his pious upbringing, would likely have
more insight into the religious mind than I.

"I don't know," said Mel. "After all, they're

Christians, belonging to an organization which publicly preaches, in the Tin Temple no less, the highest of
moral standards." This made me feel a lot better as
between strokes I viewed the distant shoreline. But
then Mel added, "That's what really has me worried!"

Stealing the Wedges

Hal Sisson

Kids were remarkably free to pursue their own whims at the beach in the thirties. Parents would assign morning chores like chopping kindling, emptying the water tray under the icebox or sweeping the mouse droppings out the back door and resetting the traps. One of the big chores was carrying buckets of water from the nearest tap to replenish the supply in the tank back at the cottage. Once the work was done, the kids disappeared.

Some played tennis on the courts right next to the railway tracks, or went to the nine-hole, sand-green golf course on the flat rim of the valley, where they hunted for bone tees or golf balls in the tall prairie wool of the rough. Others caught minnows at the lakeshore, then fished for pickerel and jackfish from an old boat or raft made of driftwood and old railway ties. You could walk the train tracks to Kell's Ravine,

Grand Slide and the Giant's Chair in one direction or Frog Pond in the other.

If it rained, you repaired to someone's cottage and played Monopoly, or records with hits like *String of Pearls, Stairway to the Stars* or *Nothing Could be Finer Than to Sneak Right up Behind Her.* Or you could go to the hub of activity at the beach—the store—and sit around matching pennies or telling jokes at one of the tables while drinking cream soda, Orange Crush or Coke, bugging each other, the storekeeper and the other customers who were doing the same thing.

You could go down to the lakefront railway station and meet the train, a real steam job that came in about ten every morning and stopped at the lengthy platform of heavy timbers to drop off mail, freight and groceries for the store. People from every cottage would be there, and you'd know just about everyone who came and went.

You could help load the grocery supplies onto the flat cart that carried the freight up the winding dirt road to the store. If you did that, the driver—a young university student whose summer job was beach caretaker—would let you ride on the wagon or even stand up front with him right behind the horse. We always said, "What's the difference between a war horse and a dray horse?" Then provided the answer, "The war horse darts into the fray!"

Parents seldom knew what their kids were up to or where they were during a day at the beach, except of course that they might actually be down at the beach, swimming, diving and lying about on the sand getting the suntan that's now considered so bad for your skin. You could just do whatever came to mind.

That freedom really impressed my grandchildren

sixty years later, when my wife and daughter and I took them to the beach. The kids had been to much more luxurious places and exotic locations, but they had a really good time at the beach. They could leave the cottage by themselves and go to the store or for a swim, something they couldn't do anywhere else.

When I was a kid at the beach, our after-supper entertainment, before the descending dark and the brightly shining stars brought about the nightly campfire and singalong, was to play Steal the Wedges.

All the kids, young and old, would gather on the beach. The game started with someone's ass dragging. The big kids would grab one of the small ones by the feet and drag his bum across the sand from the trees to the water's edge. Then they'd throw him into the lake. It wasn't cruelty, because he had to wash the sand out of his shorts anyway. This was more fun when you got old enough to be the dragger and not the draggee.

The result was a deep line in the sand across the centre of the beach. About thirty yards in either direction from this line, we'd pile up a mound of sand and create a shallow, moat-like depression around it. The playing field was sort of like a hockey rink or football field with goals or goalposts at each end but no specific boundaries. If there were sixteen players to a team after the captains chose up sides, then sixteen wedges or sticks were stuck into the mounds of sand.

Players had to make forays into enemy territory without being touched by one of the opposition and steal one of their wedges. If successful, you were allowed to return unmolested with the wedge to your own mound of sand. But if you were touched with two hands by one of your opponents in their territory, then you immediately became one of them and had to play on their side. This made for an ever-changing makeup and numbers on each side, with corresponding changes in tactics. One team would become so outnumbered that they could no longer protect their own wedges or steal from the other side, so they'd be wiped out and would lose the game. The two-handed touch rule was instituted because it was too easy to make a dive and slap a leg or some other part of the passing anatomy with one hand.

Sand was ideal for the game, as it made all falls relatively painless. Smaller boys and girls usually milled around fruitlessly, gradually learning the game. Teenagers became very adept at open field running, adopting evasive patterns to elude their equally avid pursuers; so much so that one boy at least later made the Regina Roughriders football team as an end.

A lot of people of that era would remember Kick the Can as their game of preference, but I liked Steal the Wedges best. I doubt they play it now at Lumsden Beach; maybe it was just a game of the thirties that died with the war and that generation. Thank God we didn't have television then and were able to make our own entertainment.

Frog Pond–Going, Going, Gone

Hal Sisson

I've been back to Lumsden Beach since my childhood. Some things have remained almost the same, but others have changed completely.

On one trip, I was enjoying a mid-morning stroll at the beach on a Saturday. The sun bathed the wild red rosehips and shimmering silver wolf willow. It was September, the end of the summer and the hills were ablaze with colour. It was a perfect day for a walk along what used to be the railroad tracks running north. That entire rural line has been ripped up, and the area along the lake declared Canada's narrowest and longest heritage park, stretching from Valeport to wherever the trains had at one time left Last Mountain Lake and headed north-west to Saskatoon.

I had only meant to go as far as Frog Pond, maybe as far as Buena Vista. The bees hummed and the cobalt-blue dragonflies mated as they flew and a myriad of birds sang. The steel rails, on which we used to see how far we could walk without falling off, and the ties were gone, leaving the right-of-way as a footpath partially grown over with wildflowers, grass and prairie bushes. With the immediately adjacent lake, the area was a haven for Western birds and a veritable bird-watcher's mecca and delight.

As I approached Frog Pond, one familiar noise was missing from when I'd walked the same route in my youth. From a quarter mile away, you used to hear the frogs croaking. Literally millions of them, of all sizes. The pond was about a mile north of Sunday Beach at the end of a wide ravine in the hills surrounding the lake. A stream from a spring somewhere up a gully between the hills had been slowed down by the railroad's right-of-way along the lakefront. But there was a culvert under the right-of-way, which fed the shallow, marshy pond where the waters of the lake and stream mingled.

This swampy area abounded in seaweed and other aquatic plant life, and was surrounded by bulrushes and pure unadulterated muck, full of insects. You could circle and wade to your heart's content as you caught innumerable frogs in nets and jars to take back to the beach or your cottage, to keep as pets, release in the lake, use in jumping contests or stuff down your kid brother's shorts.

The pond, covering several acres and surrounded by hills and a variety of trees—poplar, saskatoon, rose, aspen, you name it—was an environmental treasure worth preserving, and it certainly bespoke the state of the natural world in southern Saskatchewan. As kids, we were more interested in the frogs, but I can remember the hundreds of shades of green that were part of the frog pond scene. A small herd of cattle roamed the ravine, so there was some pollution from that source, but it was natural and nothing that couldn't be absorbed by the marshland and used as nutrient.

That was in the 1930s, and I believe that Frog Pond has always existed in one form or another. Certainly since the construction of the rail line, it had become an even larger pond and the most fantastic frog breeding ground our young minds could imagine.

As I approached my nostalgic goal in the late 1980s, I couldn't hear the croaking of a single frog. This was a place I remembered as one of the natural wonders of life at Lumsden Beach in the summertime. But now, not a sound. As the pond came into sight, I observed the deep brown colour of the water, devoid of any vegetation. I saw immediately what had been allowed to happen. Someone had bulldozed the culvert out of the right-of-way when they removed the railroad tracks, damming Frog Pond and killing its aquatic vegetation and amphibian denizens.

I felt sick. You don't have to be a cannibal to get fed up with people, I thought. Who in hell could be so stupid that they couldn't see the merit of leaving the pond virgo intacto? Whatever they were paid, whichever incompetents had ordered the deed only proved to me that if God hadn't wanted people to fart he wouldn't have created so many assholes. Frogs were dying all over the world, killed by human over-population and the same mentality that put the kibosh on the fisheries and clearcut the forests, and I believed Lumsden Beach and the world were the poorer for it.

I still go back to the beach from time to time, in part because I have young relatives in that region of

Saskatchewan. Sometimes my mind conjures up my siblings and old comrades kicking old road apples down a dusty trail toward me, creating a virtual return to yesteryear's pleasant summers. It may be the healthier course to search for new experiences, new friends and acquaintances and new activities and goals in life, but once in a while, "The leaves of brown come tumbling down, remember, in September" when I return once more to the happy, peaceful scene of the beach, even if only in spirit.

Sonna-Mo-Bitch

Dwayne Rowe

I grew up in northern Alberta during the forties and fifties thinking Velveeta was cheese. My Swedish uncles referred to it as endgate or bunghole, since it was highly regarded as a cure for the constant stomach flu we got from drinking alkali water from our well. Nobody had decent drinking water and dowsers had been hired, fired and beaten for their failures. Dr. Fowler's Extract of Wild Strawberry was a big seller in the general store.

One fellow had been keeping company with a young lady for several years, and each time she came down with a bout of diarrhea he would send her over some Dr. Fowler's. Their relationship came to an end, but her intestinal disorder did not. One afternoon, the erstwhile lovers met on the street and she said plaintively, "You don't send me Fowler's anymore."

There aren't that many accents in Canada, other

than in Newfoundland and Cape Breton or the Ottawa Valley. Howzit goin', eh? In Edmonton, the locals pronounce it as Emmiton and everyone knows about that place called Tronna.

In the Battle River country around Manning, Alberta, there was no accent as such, but the peculiar word usage was genuine northern Alberta slang. To complicate matters, the sizeable population of Ukrainians would superimpose their accented English onto the slang. Most people of Ukrainian ancestry could never quite get the hang of saying son of a bitch; it usually came out as sonna-mo-bitch. Mike would come out of the pool hall, look at the flat tire on his pick-me-up truck and say, "Sonna-mo-bitch!"

They could never figure out what in hell barbed wire was supposed to be called, either. I worked in the co-op store and Nick would come in and ask for "Barbara" wire or some "barber" wire. One guy even went into the barber shop looking for some. He was so embarrassed he ended up getting a haircut.

The Ukrainians would go to the lumber yard to get some "by-fours." The manager knew instantly to bring out some 2X4s. However, a new employee, who had the added handicap of not being fluent in the local dialect, was usually dumbfounded by an order for twenty by-fours. The conversation would go like this:

"Gimme twenty by-fours."

"I'm sorry, we don't have any by-fours."

"You talk-it crazy, dere's big bogger pile-it by-fours!"

"Those are 2X4s."

"Two! Sonna-mo-bitch, dere's whole bonch!"

"I know there's a whole bunch, but what size of by-fours do you want?"

"What for you ask-it by-fours, you domb bogger? By-fours is by-fours."

The rough lumber (shiplap) was called shit-lap, which, come to think of it, was pretty accurate.

"Okay, forget-it dose by-fours. Give-it to me some shit-lap."

I didn't know all that much about lumber, but I did know that the one thing you could not use shit-lap for was floor joyces. For most of my first year in English 101, I thought the author of *Ulysses* was the inventor of floor joyces.

The local merchants had three stock phrases with which to bludgeon complaining customers. If the store didn't have the requested item in the store, it was because what the customer was asking for was odd-ball. "Look," the merchant would say, like an adult talking to a child, or like a teacher talking to anybody, "what you're asking for is oddball." It could be odd-ball in size, make, colour or design.

"But I got it here last year," the customer would protest.

"Okay, lemme look," the merchant would reply. "Okay, that's not oddball, but there's been a run on those lately. Can't keep them in stock."

Now, if something wasn't oddball, and there was no run on the item but it still wasn't available, the reason given was that there was no call for that particular product. A typical exchange would go like this:

"Any flour, Mr. Jones?"

"Nope. No call for it."

"How about dill pickles?"

"Had some until the run on 'em last few days."

"What? Somebody start a rumour the pickle bank was going under?"

"Well, I got some jars out back, but you wouldn't want 'em."

"Why not?"

"They're real oddball."

Wealth accumulated in Alberta after the Leduc oil strike in 1947, but not much money found its way into new highway construction in northern Alberta until the late sixties. Before then, the Mackenzie Highway was gravel, and during the spring the retreating frost would leave the road all soft and spongy. That meant that until the roads dried out, they couldn't take the weight of the heavy trucks, so the government banned truck traffic. Locally, this period was known as the time the roads were "band."

The road "band" slowed down the economic life of the area and left truckers with free time to spend in the pool hall. There was no confusion created by the use of the phrase "there's a band on the road." Nobody ever expected a travelling band of musicians to pull into town. First off, no group had ever come, except Happy Russell's Western Show, and that was an orchestra. Also, the only local groups were the Rhythm Kings and another band headed up by Joe Becher and Fred Brick, who had been playing for dances for over thirty years. Their group was widely known and loved as Joe Pecker, Fred Prick and the Fiddling Farts.

The town council had a problem with dogs. There was no dog bylaw as such, but the common sense of the community required bitches in heat to be kept secure. The solution was obvious; they had to be spayed. The discussion would rage over the best way to spay a dog. A chap came into Fong's Cafe one morning and announced, "I finally spaded that bitch of mine."

"Didja use your jack-knife?" someone asked.

"Nope, I hit her over the head with a shovel and then dug a hole."

A few years ago a friend of mine, a provincial judge hearing a case in Manning, phoned me up to interpret some of the testimony he had heard. He read it aloud:

"These fellers came in the yard, hootin' 'n ky-iying, burnin' donuts with their light delivery and I hadda put the run on 'em. They took off in a cloud of hen shit and small stones and damn near hit the rhubarb over by the correction line."

Once I had translated the testimony, he was embarrassed by its simplicity: Some male persons, operating a pickup truck, were shouting while driving around in circles, and when the farmer appeared, the miscreants departed in a hasty manner so as to cause them to almost lose control and drive into the ditch at the point where the curvature of the earth requires that in the course of a competent and accurate survey, a quasi-artificial deviation is maintained to preserve the survey's integrity.

"Well," said the judge. "I'll be a sonna-mo-bitch."

Big Bug Wars in the West

Hal Sisson

To succeed at anything requires not just hard work but also desire, planning and plenty of strain and struggle. Even in childhood, which is often a prison existence controlled by adults, many kids know how to work toward a goal of their own devising.

At a very young age, my friend Jim Moffat strove mightily to find a solution to the grasshopper plague that had descended like an ancient curse on the drylands of the southern Prairies.

The grasshoppers of the Dirty Thirties came in all sizes to vex and torment the land, but Joe and the other kids in his gang assumed that the big ones with the largest wing span and the most powerful hind legs were both the ringleaders and the progenitors of the calamity which had beset the land. If these monsters could be eliminated, then the whole kit and kaboodle, the entire passel of loathsome creatures would go into

decline and fall, just like the Roman Empire they'd
heard about in school. To that worthy end, Jim's small
posse hunted only the really big flying bugs.

You can eat these insects; they do it in Africa.
They're a good source of protein. You can buy them
processed and dipped in chocolate in some special
gourmet shops. Jim and his friends didn't hunt
grasshoppers for the larder, though; they were a
group of vigilantes dedicated to a *cause célèbre*.

Jim's gang saw *A Tale of Two Cities* at the local
Estevan cinema in 1935, with Ronald Colman ideally
cast in the role of Sydney Carton. In Jim's fertile imagination, the hated grasshoppers assumed the villainous role played by Basil Rathbone. What stuck most in
Jim's mind about the film, though, was the use of the
guillotine during the French Revolution. When Jim
got a Meccano set that Christmas, he made a sturdy
working model of the guillotine, complete with a
weighted mechanism to which he attached one of his
father's razor blades. There was a good fifteen-inch
drop on this nasty method of execution, so it did a
very workmanlike job of beheading bugs.

The grasshoppers were accused of living off the
avails of the proletarian farmers and the boys had
heard them cursed, by no less an authority than their
parents, as dangerous sycophants who contributed
not one whit of labour toward the grain they gobbled
by the bushel. Therefore these enemies of the people
had to be brought to justice and given a short but fair
trial before their necks were placed on the block and
the razor-sharp blade of doom descended. Jim filled
small baskets with their guilty heads, to the cheers
and jeers of his peers.

It may never be known how much the efforts of

Jim and his cohorts contributed toward saving the crops and preserving the farming culture of Western Canada.

On another front, my brother Ted and I, lacking the dashing elegance and style of Jim and his band, chose another method of grasshopper decimation.

This was the era of the elastic gun. To make one, you knocked the ends out of a small wooden fruit box and sawed these into the shape of a duelling pistol. In the thirties, cars all had tires that were constantly going flat. The tires had tubes made of very elastic rubber. The term gutta percha springs to mind. You bummed old tubes from local garages and cut them into slim elastic bands, for use as ammunition.

Then you attached a clothespin firmly to the butt of the gun with one of the rubber bands and stretched another of the slim bands, tied with a knot in the middle, from the clamped clothespin to the end of the elastic gun barrel. You were then ready to shoot some other kid during the constant gang warfare, or kill large flying grasshoppers in the nearby vacant lots.

We went after the pests all afternoon one day, and that night I was awakened by the strange antics of my brother Ted. He'd sprung out of bed and was leaping around the room, sound asleep and in the throes of a nightmare. My mother came to quell the commotion and we tackled Ted, waking him up and out of his misery. He had dreamed he was grasshopper, and I must say, his imitation was very convincing.

We all did our bit, and our best, in the big bug wars of the West.

Closely Watched Birds

Hal Sisson

Do me a favour, son, don't call me Gramps, okay? You've had a chance to look the place over. Whaddaya think of the Resthaven Home for old farts? Like to live here? Didn't think so.

Why don't you take a walk down to the lounge? There's a fridge down there where those of us who are incarcerated in this here hoosegow can keep stuff. I've got a carton of fudgsicles down there with my name on it. I could use one and I know you could, too, right? Ain't supposed to eat 'em, but who gives a damn? I'll wait right here, I ain't goin' anywhere. Unfortunately.

Taste good, don't they? What were we talking about? Oh, yeah, the birds. Now as I was saying, two tons a year is a lot of sunflower seed to feed to a flock of evening grosbeaks. In your average backyard, that is. But this yard of mine was maybe larger than average. That flock ran around a hundred birds. Well, they didn't run. Maybe I should say they flew around a hundred. Don't mean the speed, although they do go damned fast. Maybe I should say they went like sixty, but that phrase would date me, wouldn't it?

Expressions come and go in the language, the slang changes. Maybe you're too young to notice that. In my day, when something was real slick and groovy, they'd say, "Boy, she kisses like sixty." No, you wouldn't remember, how could you? That's a long time ago, boy, so you have to take my word for it.

Where was I? Oh, yeah, I was thinking about the birds. Those grosbeaks that used to fly around my yard. In my mind's eye I can see those black and yellow beauties sail across the yard from one bird feeder to the other. Boy, could they eat up a storm!

But they did have their problems. Those hooked beaks of theirs are only designed to crack open certain kinds of seeds. They can't peck like chickens or most other kind of birds. Only other thing I ever saw them eat were those winged seeds that grow on the maple trees. Maybe they eat berries; yes, I think so. I liked watching them eat, and fly and live it up. Bothered me, though, when they flew straight into the picture windows.

Stop lollygaggin' boy, and pay attention when I'm talking to you! Why did I like watching the birds? Well, I can tell you about it if you want to listen, because I think I know.

I can still see that metal thing in the middle of that dusty dirt road. My friend Josh was driving the pickup and I was in the passenger seat. We were comin' back from town with supplies for the camp.

"Whoa up!" I yelled, "there's something in the

road—ahead!" Josh said he didn't see no head in the road. That's the way Josh was. I told him again to stop; he drove right over top of it. I wanted to see what it was, so Josh obliged and pulled the truck to a stop, then put her in reverse and backed her up a ways.

"Hold her right there," I said, and got out and walked back along the country road. We'd been kickin' up a lot of south Saskatchewan dust as we whipped along through the dry afternoon, and it was settling all around me in a gritty grey mist when I came on this thing glinting in the sun. It was the gun barrel and working mechanism of a small Daisy .22-calibre rifle. I picked it up out of the windrow of gravel, and it seemed to be in reasonably good condition. I started back up the road to the truck, and a few yards along the weed-strewn shoulder—my eyes were a lot keener then, I could spot things better. Not like now, when I have to wear these dagnabbed glasses.

Say, boy, did you ever stop to think how smart God must have been to place your ears on the side of your head like that? If He hadn't, I'd be wearin' goggles right now, wouldn't I? The body and its parts are really strange, don't you think? Take your ears, for instance. They are one of the strangest and most useless parts of the human body. Ears are the only part of your body that, no matter how old you get, you can bend them over like this and they'll flip straight back up again. Just try that, son. That's right, bend them over and then let go. See? They spring right back into place. I'm here to tell you that for my money, the gristle is in the wrong place. I'd rather have my ears floppin'.

You know that you could cut off the meaty part of your ears and still hear? You see, boy, you could have the meaty parts somewhere else on your body. For

instance, you could have them on your chest, or down
here on your rear end. Funny thing—then you'd have
to take down your pants to hear what I'm saying to
you right now...

What's that you say? I'm not sticking to the story?
I was going down this road? Oh, yeah. In the ditch,
hung up in some Russian thistle, I spotted—say, did
you know sometimes they ate that stuff in the Dirty
Thirties? Oh, you don't want to hear about that! You
want to hear about the gun.

Well, in the ditch there was the wooden stock to
the rifle. The whole shebang must have bounced out
of some farm truck, and when it hit the road the stock
broke away and flipped into the ditch. It was split
pretty bad. I took both parts with me and got back into
the pickup with Josh.

Yeah, and then we went like sixty back to this construction camp in the black hills where we were building water reservoirs for the government. Don't ask me
why. Just a couple of cats, a truck and a small crew.
Slept in tents—Josh, myself and the straw boss,
Hogger Weston. It was a long way into town and we
had to go in for supplies and parts every few days.
That's how come we were on those dirt back roads.

I was thinking about those other birds, the hawks,
the ones they call sparrow hawks. Maybe you read in
the papers the other day where they put them on that
endangered species list. Lots of them around in those
days, not like now. Used to sit on fence posts or tele-
phone poles or in small clumps of trees, although
there's not many trees in that country, except some
around sloughs. Or they'd float around in the sky,
never move their wings for the longest time. Pretty
birds.

About the gun? Yeah. Don't suppose you been reading about the new gun registration law. No, didn't think so. Well, anyways, I fixed it up best I could back in camp. Ran some screws into the stock and taped it back onto the barrel. Wasn't great, but it looked not too bad. Seemed like it would work okay, so next time into town I bought a couple of boxes of .22 ammo. Figured to get in some target practice after work. Nothing much to do way out there on the bald prairie. No, they didn't have television. Wasn't hardly even invented then.

On the way back to camp, I saw this hawk sitting on an old haystack in a field. The gun worked. Shot it—the bird, that is—well, shot the gun, too, if you put a fine point on it. The distance was long for a .22. I was proud of that good shot and bragged about it to the others at suppertime.

A few evenings later, Hogger took the truck and the rifle for a drive. He came back with two hawks. The next week, Josh went to the city—well, it was termed a city on the Canadian Prairies in those days. In some places in the world these days, it wouldn't be considered big enough. Was called a city though, but it was really a crazy-name small town. Yeah, we're talking about Moose Jaw, Saskatchewan. In some ways, the most colourful city in the West, although those ways hardly guaranteed it much future.

They had these brothels down on River Street—no, brothels aren't soup kitchens, boy, houses of ill repute is what they were, places of recumbent refreshment, where you could do either the vertical or the horizontal foxtrot. Worked in one once, playing the piano and telling the odd story. Sort of a nookie-bookie is what I was. Well, I won't say how good I was, but people would stop what they were doing just to listen to me. I wasn't getting paid much, so I got into the barter business, and I was getting so much in trade I never really learned anything better than whorehouse piano playing. No, I can't show you, boy, we don't have a piano here now, do we?

Well, Josh drove into the city. Speaking of driving, did I ever tell you that the U-drive was originally invented in Moose Jaw? Way back in the days before there was that many cars around. True story. You see, the police chief of Moose Jaw ran one of the main madams out of town, but not far enough to put her out of business. She bought a place on a hill just outside the city limits where the chief didn't have any jurisdiction and went back into business. Got back on her back, you might say.

She kept a couple of rigs at the local livery stable. They'd leave one rig at the railway station at the head of Main Street, or you could go to their barn and they'd hitch the horses to the buggy at the stable. Then the customer jumped in and was handed the reins. The horses knew the way out to Rosie's place and they did the rest, just took you out there. First U-drive in North America. No kidding. You didn't know that, did you, son? Well, you do now. Stop interrupting me, boy, you're ruining my train of thought.

Now what was I telling you about? What about Josh? You say he was going into town? Yeah, he was. Oh, the birds, I was talking about the birds. Well, on the way back, Josh shot himself a hawk, too. And that's how it started.

Wasn't really planned or anything, no malice afore-thought, but it kinda developed into a sort of friendly competition, see who could get the most sparrow hawks. Anytime one of us took the truck out on a trip, we'd take the old beat-up .22 rifle. Wasn't hard at first, cause they were plentiful and we ran up some good scores, first one of us being ahead, then another. But then it got kinda hard, cause we hardly ever saw a hawk. Weren't hardly none around anymore. You could drive all the way to Moose Jaw and never see a sparrow hawk. Not even one floatin' gracefully in the sky.

Don't remember who won that contest, son, but I've thought on it since—a lot. And maybe that old .22 I found lyin' in the road that day didn't accidentally fall out of somebody's truck. Maybe they got smart and just up and threw the damn thing away on purpose.

You believe me about those birds? If I'm lyin' I'm dyin'. True story. Josh could tell you about it hisself, but he died a long time ago.

How'd he die, you want to know? Well, I'll tell you. There's lots of ways of dying and some of them can be pretty scary. If I tell you, it might scare the pants off you. Go ahead, you say, you don't scare easy? Okay, sure, why not? And then maybe you could do something for me. But I'll talk to you about that later.

How would you like to kick the bucket, my boy? Ah, you're way too young to even think about that. I'm the one lying here half dead already. Most of us don't have any choice how we go, but some get more choice than others. Like my friend Josh, but I'll tell you about that in a minute.

Well, maybe those endangered species are starting to fight back. Should have the right to do that, wouldn't you think? After all, we're sharing the planet with them. We're killer apes. We have all the weapons, and not just guns, either. Did you know that Orson Welles once broke wind out of a hotel window in Manhattan and killed a condor in the Andes? I read about that in a paper once, so it has to be true. Thanks for laughing; not too much of that around here, I'll tell you. Get on with it, you say? All right.

What revenge could the animals take? What could they possibly do to us? I'll tell you one thing they're doing. There are over a billion cattle in the world already, one for every four people. Each cow has four bellies. They all eat up a storm every day and the hot gas from their nether regions is going around the world in great clouds all the time.

That's what you're smelling right now—cow farts. You knew that, didn't you? No!? You thought it was me? Well, sonny, I could have thought it was you, but I knew better. It's what all of us have to smell every day. It's payback time for McDonald's, a bovine retaliation, animal revenge. And let's not forget that mad cow disease business in England. Panicked just about everybody. Now you've got to figure out whether you'd rather eat a hamburger or smoke a cigarette.

Yes, animals got to my friend Josh in the end. He was too young to die, really, but they never gave him a chance. Now you have to remember when I tell you this, that I'm figuring what must have happened from what we found later. Don't rightly know, but this is what we figured.

He was coming across the prairie one evening in early fall at dusk—you know, the time when the hills turn violet in the evening light and everything goes into a greyish haze just before dark. Can't hardly see anything clearly. He was ridin' horseback and headin' for the ranch house.

This was a long time ago, remember, when we were young and people still kept some riding horses on farms, and there was still some wild country around.

A bird, a big jeezly bird, a humongous grey owl, swooped out of the whensome and took a huge gash out of his arm. The horse spooked and threw him off. He staggered to his feet, but the bird got him again, this time sinking its claws into his head and face, maybe blinding him in one eye. He fell back into a dry gulch and bashed his head on a rock. He was knocked out cold.

Josh came to around dawn, and he heard this loud hissing. With his one good eye, he sees he's lying in a snake pit. There are snakes crawling all around him. God, they're rattlers. He lays still, but then he doesn't have much strength to do otherwise, because he's been bleeding a lot, and maybe that's what brought the vultures just after sun-up.

Yeah, that's right, boy. He's lying there in a pool of his own blood with rattlesnakes crawling over the whole area, buzzards circling overhead, and some of them sitting in a ring around him, coming closer all the time.

What would you have done, son? Death comes to us all and it isn't pretty. I don't mind dying myself, I just don't want to be there when it happens. I sure don't want to go like my friend Josh.

The vultures got him in the end, because his bones had been picked pretty clean when we found him. I'd like to think he probably had enough strength left to aggravate some of them rattlesnakes enough to get bitten several times. Better to die that way than getting eaten alive by vultures!

So, there you have it, and here I lie. You don't see any rattlesnakes around the room, do you?

Nowadays, I just go in fits and starts, have a connip-tion occasionally and go into some kinda St. Vitus's dance.

That's what I wanted to talk to you about. Do you think you could be a good boy and get me about fifty capsules of a thing called Seconal? I know your mom has some in that big medicine cabinet that she leaves full of that kind of medicinal junk. Better not bring me the whole bottle—leave a few pills in it and bring me the rest.

And go to your dad's liquor supply and bring me a bottle of Irish whiskey. Johnny Powers if he's got it, but never mind the brand, he likely only has one. And if he doesn't have that, get a bottle of scotch. Look for a Chivas Regal. Or maybe a Crown Royal rye if you see that, but none of that cheap Alberta Liquor Control Board stuff. Just don't bother telling them you're doing this for me. Naw, they'll never miss the stuff.

Why do I want these things? Good question. You'd just be doin' me a favour to help me cure these godaw-ful headaches I keep gettin' lately. Yeah, I'll tell you some more stories when you come again. But make it soon, will you? I like talkin' to you.

Say, did you ever hear the one about the guy who had these excrooshiatin' headaches? Had them since he was a young fella, about your age. Well, when he was about thirty-five he couldn't stand it anymore, so he went to see a sawbones—a doctor, to you. This doc, who had some weird theories, told him that the only sure cure for his headaches was castration. Yeah, removal of the balls. Pretty drastic, but the guy just couldn't stand these terrible headaches any longer, so he said go ahead, do it.

The operation was a success, no more headaches. He decided to celebrate by buying himself a brand new outfit—head to foot, from underwear to bow tie, a shirt, suit, shoes, socks, the works. At the men's shop they measured him for everything—forty-two tall suit, size fifteen shirt, pair of number ten brogues, and a seven and three-eighths hat.

"And you'll want a loose, baggy pair of boxer shorts," the salesman says to him. "No, I don't want boxer shorts, I always wear tight jockey shorts," says our guy. "I really think you should take the roomy boxers," the salesman says to him. "No, I want jockey shorts, like I always wore. Why should I start wearing big boxers?" "Because," the salesman says, "if you wear tight shorts it always gives you one helluva headache!"

You leavin'? Okay, 'bye kid. Don't forget to come back soon, now.

The P*** Word

Hal Sisson

History is written by the victors, they say, but it's also written by those who would sanitize events and wash out all traces of the less genteel aspects of humanity. So it was with the legend of Twelve Foot Davis, whose name became synonymous with the whole northern Peace River country.

Henry Fuller Davis was born in Vermont in 1820. He was a prospector during the California Gold Rush, then he headed north to the gold fields of the Cariboo region in British Columbia.

He was nicknamed Twelve Foot Davis after he discovered and staked a claim to a twelve-foot gap between two adjacent claims in Barkerville. Davis extracted some twenty thousand dollars' worth of gold, a fortune in those days, before selling his claim.

Davis later became a free trader, dealing in fur, foodstuffs and other goods on the Fraser and Parsnip rivers, and setting up trading posts along the Peace

River. He soon earned the enmity of the Hudson's Bay
Company. Company officials took a jaundiced view of
men like Davis, who cut into their profits by staking
newly arriving farmers, miners and other settlers to
food and trapping supplies to get them started. Davis
hated the big trading companies like the Bay,
Reveillon Freres and the North West Company with
an equal passion.

One of Davis' main trading posts was at Peace
River Landing near the confluence of the Peace and
Smoky rivers, the site of the present-day town of Peace
River. The Hudson's Bay Company had a fur trading
post on what later became the main street of the town,
where their fur storage building could be seen from
the lookout on the hill where Colonel James "Peace
River Jim" Kennedy Cornwall buried his friend Davis.
The hill, where the two men had often camped, later
became known as Twelve Foot Davis Hill.

Author James G. MacGregor describes Davis's bur-
ial spot in his history of Peace River, *The Land of Twelve
Foot Davis*: "Rising abruptly...the hill ascends many
hundred feet until it reaches its peak in a white speck.
This speck is another fenced-in-spot, the last resting
place of Twelve Foot Davis, who in life climbed to this
lofty station to admire the view, but on his death,
September 13, 1900, was buried at Lesser Slave Lake.
In 1912, in deference to his old friend's wishes, Peace
River Jim Cornwall had his bones taken up and carried to this place. As a further tribute to his old friend
and fellow trader, Colonel Cornwall caused to be
inscribed on the headstone these words: *Pathfinder,
Pioneer, Miner and Trader. He was every man's friend and
never locked his cabin door.* Twelve Foot Davis, what a
resting place you chose! If ever a spirit gains rest and

repose, yours must have done so, as from its dwelling place, day after day, it looks out over a scene so serene and a land so beautiful."

The "beautiful view" theory was repeated in more recent books about the area. Davis may have liked the site and used it to watch the river for any boats coming in with fur to sell, but that's not why his bones were interred at that spot. That's not the the way I heard it, and it's not the way MacGregor heard it, either. The dictates of public decorum kept MacGregor from telling the real story.

Sam Harris was an old-timer from the Peace River district who served as a bailiff in High Prairie where I had a once-a-week law office. I talked to him on Sept. 12th, 1957 about Twelve Foot Davis and Jim Cornwall and took notes. Sam told me he'd previously been interviewed by MacGregor. I subsequently talked to MacGregor, who confirmed that Sam had told both of us the same story.

Sam Harris didn't know Twelve Foot Davis, but he knew Colonel Jim Cornwall very well. Cornwall told Sam, "Twelve Foot Davis hated the Hudson's Bay Company. When he and I went to the lookout point, high on the hill above the town, you could clearly see the Bay's fur post in the valley below. Twelve Foot Davis asked, made me promise, to bury him at that point overlooking the town and the Bay post with his feet pointing downhill so he could 'piss on the Hudson's Bay Company.' "

Sam Harris's explanation rings true, given what is known of Davis's character and manner of speech. MacGregor told me his publishers refused to print the word *piss* or any other words relating to intimate parts of the human body and their functions. I appreciate the author's dilemma, having found that prudery still exists today. They had an easier time of it back in the thirteenth century when the word *piss* came into the English language from the old French verb *pisser*.

Until recently, unless an author wished to encounter great prejudice and court non-publication, he could not use *piss* in Canadian writing—in fact, the spellchecker on my Macintosh laptop beeps every time I type the word.

Has the pendulum swung too far? Political correctness seems to be in favour once again, forcing authors to resort to linguistic delicacy and euphemistic alternatives for four-letter words like *piss*, such as the call of nature, go, leak, see a man about a dog, piddle, powder my nose, pump ship, see a Chinaman about a flute lesson, or shake hands with the unemployed.

Ancient grade-school humour used a doubletalk version of the word in this joke, according to a 1954 book called *Rationale of the Dirty Joke*:

Knock, Knock!
Who's there?
Santa.
Santa who?
Centipede on the Christmas Tree!

Another book, *Pissing in the Snow*, first printed in 1977, points out the perils of linguistic squeamishness: "A boy is told by his mother to say *whisper* instead of *piss*; however, the father is not informed of the code, and when the boy says he wants to whisper, the father invites him to do it in his ear."

Piss. A perfectly good word. You hear it all the time. I think I'll go have one.

English as Another Language

Dwayne Rowe

The English language, as written by Robertson Davies, Alice Munro or Carol Shields or as spoken by Rex Murphy or William F. Buckley, is a wondrous thing. But in comparison with the special talent of my wife Roseanne, those extraordinarily gifted individuals continue to utilize the standard tools of their craft, albeit elegantly. They have not demonstrated a capacity to depart from the norm, to ignore existing boundaries, to soar freely, unbounded by convention and thereby elevate their audience another dimension within the universe of human communication. With Roseanne, it is as though certain words and phrases are transmitted in a burst like a laser beam through a prism.

I noticed this facet of Roseanne's personality when she was attempting to deal with our three unruly teenage daughters. She had reached the breaking point and finally hollered, "If the three of you don't smarten up, you are both going to bed." A few days later, when the girls complained there wasn't enough variety in the home-made lunches they were forced to take to school and that they were sick and tired of eating Velveeta sandwiches, Roseanne reminded them that we were not made of money and admonished the girls to take into account that "cheese is one of your cheaper forms of meat."

I began jotting down these spontaneous statements and one day, when I made fun of her penchant for uttering bizarre phrases, she outright threatened me, inquiring whether I would like "a punch between the nose." On another occasion when I was bugging her, she arched her eyebrows and uttered this icy warning: "Stop that or I'll punch your lights in." In a fast food restaurant, I made her laugh while she was drinking a soda and she asked me never to do that again because the fizzy mixture went down her nose.

It didn't take long before her close friends began collecting these Roseanne-isms and we would pass them around when we met or share them by mail or phone—the dinosaur days before the Internet and e-mail.

Roseanne was at a summer retreat with her friend Jeannette and they both participated fully in the daytime activities, but when members of the study group were about to embark on an evening stroll, Roseanne declined to join them, explaining, "My stamina comes in short bursts." Another time, she answered an inquiry as to her general health by stating that "Every day I wake up with or without a headache." On matters of health, Roseanne had a variety of theories which would erupt spontaneously when attempting, as always, to help other people. She once advised a friend, who was in the midst of a horrendous coughing attack, "I think you need an expectorant." Another friend was embarking on yet another attempt at losing weight and Roseanne calmly explained that a lifestyle change was more appropriate than any fad diet but in the meantime, perhaps it would be wise for her to "have your toast without jam and bread."

I asked Roseanne why our friend Sylvia was no longer attending Weight Watchers and was informed that, alas, the lovely Sylvia had somehow "forgotten to renew her Lifetime Membership."

No aspect of health care escaped Roseanne's field of expertise. In assisting an acquaintance who was interested in beginning a regimen of daily vitamin intake, Roseanne recommended Vitamin E, but only on condition that it contained "a high level of BTUs."

One night, she informed me that scientists had developed a new wonder drug to "prevent anti-aging." She was quite surprised when I told her I wasn't interested. She also brought me up to date on the spread of AIDS, which seemed to be "prevalent among homophiliacs." Before my own troubles with clogged arteries, Roseanne had advised an elderly friend to avoid the pain of angina attacks by putting nitrogen under his tongue. That, I suppose, could be an effective remedy provided it wasn't in liquid form, as even to veterans of a typical northern Alberta winter, a blast of absolute zero in the facial area tends to be a bitch.

My cousin Brian is a dentist and Roseanne decided she would suggest that her mother consider replacing a set of dentures, because "her teeth are on their last legs." She also informed me that some people get "chest pains" in their back or in their stomach. Despite its transmogrified form, that is correct advice, since angina can manifest itself in various parts of the body.

In the last fifteen years or so, I've tried to eat a healthy breakfast. and one morning I asked whether there were any berries left to sprinkle on top of my bran flakes. "No," was Roseanne's curt reply, "cereal season is over."

The Grande Prairie region was a fabulous place to pick all sorts of lovely, ripe, fat berries, including the wondrous saskatoon. We had made a terrific haul one afternoon and I was cleaning the berries by picking out twigs and sorting out the green ones, when Roseanne instructed me not to throw away the wrinkled ones because she could "use them to make raisins." One afternoon, I came home from work, hungry as usual, and was cutting myself a slice of gorgeous lemon pie. Roseanne came in the kitchen and said in her usual gentle tone, "I don't think it's good for you to drink so much pie." I certainly had to agree; that meringue really sticks to the lips when you try to guzzle it down, even using a beer mug.

Then there was that afternoon when she received another nagging reminder from the hospital to come in for what she referred so as a "mammy-o-gram." When I suggested she should make an immediate appointment for the examination—and could perhaps save on gas by car pooling with Aunt Jemima—this led to me sleeping with one eye open for about a week, like a New Yorker visiting Toronto, until the threat of random attack had subsided.

There was the perennial problem of alcohol abuse in smaller communities and it was Roseanne's opinion that "it's better to check into a treatment centre before you're dead." The scourge of Alzheimer's disease was becoming the subject of media coverage, and Roseanne told me flat out that she hoped to be dead before her mind started to deteriorate. I couldn't disagree, because studies show that after death the human brain turns to mush rather quickly, particularly for avid fans of soap operas or *Entertainment Tonight,* since they have the advantage of a healthy head start.

I don't know whether it's a special form of extrasensory perception, but one day my lovely wife informed me that she was experiencing "an impending sense of panic." We waited and waited, but nothing came of it except that afterwards, we felt strangely rested and refreshed.

Another time, just before we retired for the evening, she sighed, "I hope I never again have a day like tomorrow." That's a nice twist on the defiant utterance of the ever-determined Scarlett O'Hara, and because I also knew what the morrow would bring, I could not disagree. Like Scarlett, Roseanne has a fine fashion sense, so in order to reward herself—if we survived that day—she vowed to "buy a red or blue blouse that isn't white."

We did persevere, life went on and soon it was the Christmas season and we were hurrying to send off presents, including a custom-designed large candy cane to my mom, who lived in Sweden. Roseanne was supervising the process and warned me, "Be careful how you wrap it so if it breaks it will arrive in one piece." I urged her to send off resumés to Canada Post and some of the nationally known courier companies, but she declined on the basis that she wanted to spend more time with the children.

Roseanne had an innovative sense, even though she was often shy on the details of where, as we all know, the devil resides. Because I often got lost when we were driving around and like any real man, refused to stop and ask directions since to do so would relegate me to the category of baby robin, jam tart and wuss, Roseanne suggested that we purchase a compass magnet that would stick to the dashboard with a magnet. "Good idea," I said, "if you want to go on a Sunday drive in Lethbridge and end up in Yellowknife."

One time we were touring the countryside with my dad behind the wheel of his new car. Roseanne pointed to some windmills in a field that were just standing there with their blades absolutely still. Since my father was a high school math and science teacher and possessed a keen, logical mind, Roseanne decided to posit this theory: "When there's no wind, why not have a small auxiliary motor to keep them turning?" My poor old dad nearly drove into the ditch before he got himself under control.

Roseanne was ahead of her time; I'm positive there's a multi-billion-dollar federally funded project to store—underground in humongous batteries—electricity produced by solar panels, the sole purpose of which is to provide sufficient electrical energy to power small motors to turn windmills on those rare windless days in Québec.

Roseanne always had a keen eye for public safety. She once told a visitor not to go swimming at certain Victoria beaches because "the chloroform count is too high." All in all, I'd suggest that's damn fine advice, because falling sound asleep in crap-infested waters is one sure way to botch an otherwise enjoyable visit to the Island. Roseanne was always ready to help out tourists. She advised one American couple, "Don't stop at the summit, the view isn't very good."

During a summer storm when high winds came up unexpectedly, Roseanne issued a bulletin to some nearby campers to watch out for falling branches as they could be real "widow-killers." It had the desired effect because at the neighbouring campsite, five obviously mature ladies picked up their knitting and jumped into their RV. Cousin Brian built a house on Pender Island and Roseanne, while talking to a realtor, stated that it had a "three hundred and sixty-five-degree view." "That's great," replied the agent. "If Linda Blair (how soon we forget, but she was that Satan-possessed gal in *The Exorcist*) is ever looking for a house, I'll know where to go."

In response to prairie folk who would make light of the supposed huge amounts of annual precipitation falling on Vancouver Island, Roseanne would zing them with the irrefutable declaration that "a lot of people don't know this, but Edmonton gets more rain per capita than Victoria." I always suspected the Alberta capital had a lot of soggy-minded people, but I could never put my finger on the source. Once, when asked about the whereabouts of a certain person, Roseanne said, "Oh, he's still in Edmonton but now he's dead." I have lived in Edmonton and sometimes that distinction has to be made.

After moving to beautiful Sidney-by-the Sea on the Island in 1984, we would drive around looking at interesting properties, but they were either too small or too big and expensive. Roseanne came home one day, excited, to inform me she had found the perfect place that was "two acres by two acres."

At the petting zoo in Beacon Hill Park in Victoria, Roseanne pointed out a magnificent bird to a visitor saying, "Look, there's a male peacock." Today, what with the dramatic revelations of sexual preference by various hens, cocks, chicks and clucks, that precise categorization is more commonly heard.

Roseanne's friend Molly Phillips was eighty-four when she went with Roseanne to China on an extensive trip. Molly was an author, teacher and perennial traveller, a virtual dynamo who astounded everyone with her energy and vibrant lifestyle. One day, after spending an exhausting day with Molly, Roseanne said wistfully, "I would love to know the secret of her longlivity."

Then there was her astute identification of the religious affiliation of a neighbour who, replete with the obligatory bulging tool belt, worked as a multi-talented handyman. She described him to me as "a senior member of the Utilitarian church." After that, I always thought of the chap as Deacon Butt-Crack.

As sometimes happens, a couple we were good friends with were in the process of getting divorced, and Roseanne and I attempted to remain neutral. As time progressed, we saw quite a bit of the wife and Roseanne suggested we should make a point of having the husband over for dinner as otherwise, "it will seem like we're osterizing him." I couldn't go through with the invitation, because every time I saw this poor chap, I'd be imagining him going around and around, trapped inside that famous brand-name blender, being mercilessly chopped, diced and puréed.

On a trip to Vancouver, we were in a hotel room watching an episode of *Murder, She Wrote*. The opening scene featured a man—extremely dead—lying on the living room floor. Roseanne didn't wait for Angela Lansbury; she solved the matter in an instant, announcing, "I bet he killed himself." At the time, there was some sort of economic conference in Vancouver, and she dismissed that august gathering of gurus by stating, "These people spend way too much time in their little Eiffel towers." One economic forecaster was known for his gloomy prognostications and Roseanne labelled him as "a Joe Blitzkrieg with that black cloud over his head."

Travelling with Roseanne was always fun. As we were about to depart our hotel in Paris on Rue de Bellechasse (or, as she referred to it, Rudy something) she told me: "Don't forget your portable camera." Obviously that was the right choice, as opposed to the stationary one, embedded in cement, back home.

Once, I was flying one-way from Victoria to Kelowna and Roseanne was going to drive there later in the week to pick me up. Before I left, she insisted that I leave her a copy of my itinerary.

On another trip, Roseanne and I were driving back to London, Ontario from Kitchener-Waterloo and because we had skipped lunch, we were starting to feel a bit peckish. We had deliberately avoided Highway 401 in favour of a series of secondary roads that seemed to be lacking in the usual clusters of roadside restaurants. We continued on, discussing simple pleasures like a cup of coffee and a doughnut, when Roseanne had an inspiration. "How about we stop at one of those places named after that dead Canadian hockey player?" Unfortunately, some things are not meant to be and we didn't see a Tim Horton's until the next day, when we were somewhere in darkest Mississauga.

When Hal Sisson and I decided to write our first collection of short stories, Roseanne offered some good advice: "Even though you have talent," she warned me, "you must have discipline to be a writer. Remember, you're no Eleanor Parker." I could not disagree with that blunt assessment and regret that I never did receive an invitation to chow down with Eleanor—or Robert Mitchum, one of her co-stars— and the usual crew around the illustrious Round Table at the rear of the MGM cafeteria.

Roseanne ran a finely-tuned household and her constant philosophy was that "Every day you should do a little, major job." She believed strongly that this could be accomplished by average persons "even though they often tend to be mediocre." Different points of view were encouraged as well as analysis of viable options. As Roseanne discussed various courses of action with one of her friends, she would conclude, "A , you could go there right away, or C..." In weighing an alternative proposal, Roseanne would issue her assessment: "You may be right, but on the same hand..."

Discussions would sometimes turn to matters of home security and how one could present a profile that would discourage a home invasion. One tactic was the pretense of owning a trusty canine for protection, since it's well known that most bad guys are afraid of attack hounds.

Roseanne's scenario—as explained to her friend Sylvia—unfolded in this way: "If I opened the door and Clifford Olson was standing there, I would say 'just a minute while I tie up my dog.' " Unfortunately for Sylvia, when she's having dinner with a group and the serious topic of reinstating capital punishment is introduced—inevitably followed by someone nominating Clifford Olson as the first candidate—she is wont to burst out laughing and has to leave the table.

Those remaining, particularly the ones who adhere to the stern precepts of the Alliance Party, are not amused. I have advised Sylvia to blame her outrageous behaviour on an uncontrollable spasm caused by transitory Tourette's syndrome, but she is inexplicably reluctant to trust me in these matters.

Roseanne opened a travel accessory and gift shop in Sidney some years ago. Since she stocked an array of luggage, I suggested we could give one of our daughters, at wholesale, a nice suitcase for a Christmas present. Roseanne declined, saying, "Let's wait until she settles down and quits travelling so much." I came into the shop one day as she was instructing an employee to "make sure you wipe off that merchandise; it's covered in rain dust." Later, Roseanne explained the store return policy to the novice clerk who was dealing with a customer. "Give her the same thing," counseled Roseanne, "but don't charge her the difference."

A dear friend of ours has one of those amazing, striking, strong-featured faces, and Roseanne explained it as being due to the fact that "he's part Métis." As opposed to full-blooded Métis, I guess. One time after we had returned from sailing, a customer pointed out that Roseanne's lower forehead area appeared to be sunburned. To this day, none of us know the reason behind Roseanne's bizarre response when she explained matter-of-factly, "I forgot to put after-shave on my eyelids."

By now, you're probably attempting to come up with a theory as to how this sort of phraseology can issue from the lips of this delightful woman, in the sense that a sunny April day can burst forth with a dazzling sixty-second shower of perfect raindrops.

The research I've undertaken has led me to the following hypothesis: Roseanne is an avid – although inadvertent – practitioner of the rare art of the Irish Bull. The *American Heritage Dictionary of the English Language*, Fourth Edition, 2000, defines Irish Bull in this way: "A statement containing an incongruity or a logical absurdity, usually unbeknown to the speaker; 'with a pistol in each hand and a sword in the other' is an example of an Irish bull."

Roseanne is one of two daughters of the late, lovely Anne Conroy, a Maureen O'Hara type with flaming red hair and a temper to match. One way to get Anne boiling was to call her Annie. Anne's mother left Ireland during WWI to visit a relative in Scotland and Anne was born in that country. When people learned of this event they would say to Anne, "But, you must be Scottish, not Irish." And Annie Conroy would snort and strike a near-mortal blow with this rhetorical challenge: "If kittens were born in the oven, would you be callin' them biscuits?"

Even though about fifty percent of Roseanne's DNA is composed of Swedish blood—as opposed to thirty-seven-point-five percent for myself—it was the Irish side of her overall essence that came to the fore in the critical aspect of communication, leading, I believe, to her intermittently odd manner of speech.

I must point out that the examples I've given arrive totally out of the blue; you can't make them up, nor can she. They only occur in the presence of family or friends when she's totally relaxed but, like most women, is still multi-tasking, either in fact or in thought. The phenomenon never visits her in the course of the dozens of presentations she gives before small or large gatherings or at business meetings, or during her frequent appearances on television or radio to offers up excellent advice to the travelling public. It's a delight we've all learned to accept.

To this day, when Roseanne utters another Roseanne-ism, I'll reach for my cell phone and call Brian or Sylvia or Harry or someone else who wishes to share in the joy of those unusual phrases that—transcendentally—are always based in reason and accurately reflect the purpose of the speaker.

I have long accused Roseanne of being a Luddite, as she does not cotton to computers or electronic messaging. There is some hope, however. She informed me the other day that perhaps it was time for her to learn how to use the computer so she could get "my own e-mail number." When I regretted not having made arrangements with the minions at the Shaw television empire to obtain another tier of programming so I could get the proper channel to watch Lance Armstrong win his fourth consecutive Tour de France, Roseanne hinted that might not be a problem next year. If I was a very good boy, then for Christmas she just might buy me one of those newfangled cable dishes.

The Horseshoe Valley News

Hal Sisson

I once spent a few weeks reading old issues of a northern Saskatchewan weekly newspaper, covering just over a year in the mid-fifties. The rural news encompassed some communities so deep in the boondocks that the first thing a housewife did before breakfast was sweep the beaver farts out of the kitchen. I could have picked Dancing Hills, Blue Sky, or Hay Lakes, but I remember with particular affection one rural correspondent from a place called Horseshoe Valley.

Nov. 27—Wm. D. Blenkinsop was busy making a new dray top on his truck for pulp hauling. Mrs. Blenkinsop Sr. attended the monthly missionary meeting at the Baptist Church. The quality wedding of the fall season was the Sherstibitoff-Cockburn nuptials (reported elsewhere) held at the same church. Our best wishes to Nellie and congratulations Billy Cockburn.

Bad curve on the Rock Ravine Road hill by the post office has certainly proved a real danger to strangers to the district. At least three cars coming from the oil well site have gone over the edge in the last two weeks—fortunately without too much damage. Maybe some warning signs should be erected. However, the sanitation inspector of the Peace River Health Unit wasn't so lucky on Thursday. Having previously been warned verbally about the hill, he rounded the curve cautiously only to have a flat tire throw him into a skid and over he went. He wasn't hurt but the car was damaged so badly it had to be towed to Grande Prairie.

Mar. 4—Cockburns off on wedding trip. Bad roads and weather on Pig Day. Roads are badly drifted with a blizzard tonight. If this isn't the worst hog shipping week, the baddest one ever, I should hope to kiss a pig. Hogs will have to be taken to the railroad twenty-six miles distant, by team, due to road conditions.

The annual school meeting was held Wednesday but no one attended. Over the weekend the thermometer reading was minus 36.

Seen—Pop Blenkinsop, Jim and Mickey Moffat with the four grays, hauling the car home. Aunt Elly Joan all on her lonesome doing chores.

March 18—With Easter so close, it seems the pretty chickadees are heralding the greatest event of the Christian era. Soon we shall see the results of Easter's awakening. The hall has been wired for lights. The show last week, *No Leave, No Love*, starring Van Johnson, Keenan Wynn and Pat Kirkwood, had a better attendance, but we can do better yet with *Girl of the Limberlost*, starring Ruth Nelson and Loren Tindall. Also *The March of Time*.

Little Billie Seaman is spending a few days at the camp, where Mildred is cooking for Ray's men. He is having a swell time, and so is Mildred. Billy Blenkinsop sawed wood for the Wickwire family Monday, and for Claude and the home farm Wednesday.

Seen—Bob Nutter rushing to Grande Prairie to get some teeth out. Pete Swinghammer of Little Meadows was here Tuesday to find a carpenter. No luck. Aunt Elly Joan shearing sheep for Pop Blenkinsop. Don and Linc Weaver and crew passed through Monday. Pop Blenkinsop and Mike Delano came home with loads on.

WHAT AND WHERE IS HELL?

That Burning Question Answered

- is it a farce or a furnace?
- how long will it last?
- will it burn out?

Hear these questions answered by Evangelist F. E. JOHNSON

Singing - 7.30 p.m.
Lecture - 7.45 p.m.
SUNDAY, APRIL 14th
COMMUNITY HALL

April 1—Neil McLean is home at Gus Lovelock's after spending five weeks in hospital. He cannot walk yet, but he can run. Stan says it won't be long before he will be on his feet again. Mr. George Wickwire is suffering from his fall and lung trouble. Gordie

Johnson hurt his foot while helping load pulp near Jackfish Lake; he jabbed a pick into his instep. He isn't worried none about catching an infection, as he says meat always keeps good in the winter.

March went out and April came in with the roar of a lion, with temperatures down, heavy snow and winds. Easter Sunday morning was one of undescribable beauty in the surrounding landscapes.

Heavy frost did its best in amazing patterns on the trees and shrubbery. Truly one could not look at such beauty without pausing to think of all Easter Morn means—new hopes, renewed faith in the Divine Plan of our Heavenly Father. The Zaborski boys visited Rosebud and the Blenkinsops Sunday, while Louis Blenkinsop had the misfortune to cut cut his hand while chopping wood. Aunt Elly Joan rested there Saturday night.

This was surely April Fool's Day, judging by the weather. The roads are bad and the men have plenty of shovelling.

April 22nd—Grandma Wickwire celebrated her seventy-fifth birthday anniversary March 26th. Grandma's anniversary was Good Friday this year, the one and only time it has occurred on Good Friday in all the years. She says there are four ages in life: childhood, youth, middle age and "you're looking good!"

Seen—Aunt Elly Joan with a little pig on the stone boat. Pop Blenkinsop with a heavy load on. Little Billie Seaman busy making a baby crib. Mildred setting the New Hampshires. Rocky Glen Acorn has the cast on his leg which was broken.

Church bulletin: At the service this Sunday, the sermon topic will be "What is Hell?" Come early and listen to our choir practice. Stay late and take Bingo lessons.

April 29—A number of farmers received baby
chicks several weeks ago and the beekeepers are looking for their bees this week. The roads are bad and it
is hard to decide which mode of travel to try, neither
sleigh nor wagon being very good. Daisy Day visited
his parents at Dawson Creek over the weekend. While
there he attended the amateur hour; said some were
able, some unable and some lamentable.

May 14—The Nutters and the Zaborskis received
their bees Monday. A bee stung Aunt Elly Joan and
she demanded that something be done about it. Zeke
Zaborski promised that if they find that bee, they will
do something. The muskrat trappers are moving to
their trapping ground, hoping for a good catch.

All the families, including the two lovely little children, Rosebud and Tulipbud, were present at the
farm. Soup Campbell arrived in time for supper. The
frogs are definitely caroling the spring. Down the lane
something stirred, was it a bird stirred? Pop

Blenkinsop went to Beaverlodge yesterday for gas, returning this evening really gassed up.

Seen—Mildred, Louise, Rosebud and Tulipbud going to the post office and jubilant over their baby chicks. Aunt Elly Joan, who is a hospital patient, is much improved in health.

Farming is in full swing and farmers haven't time to breathe or sleep.

June 3rd—We have had lovely farming weather all week. The sun is shining, birds are singing, buds of trees are breaking with lovely little fresh green leaves appearing. God's beautiful nature is wonderful and one just loves to be outside.

Saturday evening, Sid Kahnoff brought Aunt Elly Joan home from hospital. Louis Blenkinsop came along, too. Mildred visited Aunt Elly Joan Monday. Rosebud stayed with Grandma. Judith Nutter spent Wednesday with Aunt Elly Joan. Mildred had an ice cream treat Wednesday evening.

Back of the loaf is the snowy flour, and back of the flour are the mills, back of the mill is the wheat and the shower and the sun, and the Father's will.

The Woman's Auxiliary met at Denise Kit's Wednesday afternoon. The roll call was answered with rags for a rug. Mom Blenkinsop to hook the rug as she is one of the best hookers in the country. After the correspondence was attended to, everyone got busy tying the comforter.

June 9—The Mounties state that a bear is suspected of breaking and entering the pigpen at the Rainbow Mission, by night, with felonious intent to commit an indictable offence. They mauled and mangled a large sow and six other pigs. Three of them died the next morning and others may do so. No charges have as yet been laid, as the Mounties are also considering pigslaughter. The Zaborskis have thirty-one lambs. Judith Nutter is home again minus her tonsils. She spent last week in hospital.

June 16—On Sunday the Pobudas, Olsons and Nutters visited Stony Beach. The children enjoyed the picnic and the trip, excepting for dust and mosquitoes, which, however, are to be found everywhere. Bobbie Philipps lost a pig to the bears last week. Zaborkis lost one pig. The bear population is increasing rapidly, and we can barely stand it. Several bears with three bear cubs have been seen, so they will bear watching.

July 1—Seen—Jimmy and Mom walked down to visit Aunt Elly Joan last evening. Mrs Higginbottom and Merrill Roseworm of Clear Hills visited Aunt Effie last week.

Birthday greetings to Pop Blenkinsop who celebrated another milestone June 21. In honour of the occasion, Tulipbud made ice cream and her special raspberry meringue cake and decorated it with fifty-eight cherries, each cherry denoting a milestone. One would have difficulty proving the contrary, as Pop says the church that had the record of his birth burned down in 1920. Pop was impressed by the well-stocked table, because he said he could remember when he had to use water on his cornflakes.

Willie Wickwire was on the sick list. He's been working like a plough horse and needs relaxation. Bob Phillips came up to sample the food, and brought back a borrowed book of verse. It was a rare volume—a borrowed book that comes back. The sad news was received in the community this week, that Joe Warren had passed on to his reward after a long illness. Joe once admitted to being his own worst enemy, but his wife said, "Not while I'm alive, you're not." He had no last words to say before he died. His wife was with him till the end.

WHO HAS MY GUN?

Someone borrowed my gun—a Winchester 12-gauge pump—from me or Manley Hillman. Would the person who borrowed it please return it to me as I need it.

J.D. Levesque
Peace River

August 12—Gigi Whilakers took the ladies to Sexsmith. Mrs. Paul Blenkinsop received second prize for the crocheted bedspread, while Mrs. Wm. D. Blenkinsop received first prize for a hooked rug. Quite a few Horseshoe Valley folks took in the showing of Ben Hur in Grande Prairie. Little Bobbie Slemon said he liked Ben but hated Hur.

We had a cloudburst this afternoon followed by hail, followed by Pop Babcock coming home with a load on. Mrs. Arnott used to have a lovely field of oats, which she had sowed herself.

Seen—Aunt Elly Joan looking anxiously for mail. Mildred, Louise and Rosebud going to the post office on the tractor.

Wild fruit is plentiful and everyone is busily picking raspberries and saskatoons.

August 12th—Government veterinarians were in the district last week testing for Bang's disease. Haying has commenced in the haying meadows where hay is very good. So, hey, nonny, nonny!

Several car and truck trades this week. Herbie Bekevich exchanged his old truck for a new one, and Leo Ouellette exchanged his truck for a car. Jim Robertshaw has gone to Edmonton to receive medical and dentist treatment. The six members of the Lone Patrol, a junior branch of the Junior Forest Wardens, met with Assistant Ranger Russ Nutter on Sunday to discuss various aspects of their project. Sammy Friedman spent several days in Providence Hospital after having the misfortune to cut one of his fingers off while splitting wood. They couldn't sew it back on, so he gave the finger to the Hospital.

October 14th—Thanksgiving was quiet this year. We wonder if we as a nation should stop to give thanks and gratitude to God, as did the American Pilgrim Fathers for the first harvest in 1621. Sunday visitors at Aunt Elly Joan's were Uncle Jack, Mrs. Higginbottom and Tulipbud.

Seen—Smiling Chet Gilmour, Dave Eustace, and Noel Lamoose going to Sexsmith; Rosebud and Tulipbud visiting Grandma Blenkinsop.

I AM STILL LOOKING FOR MY GUN!

Someone borrowed my gun—a Winchester 12-gauge pump—from me or Manley Hillman. Would the person who borrowed it please return it to me as I need it.

J.D. Levesque
Peace River

Nov. 4—The W.I. held its monthly meeting at the home of Mrs. Blenkinsop Sr. Wednesday afternoon.

After the final details were attended to tickets were passed and Judith Nutter held the lucky number, receiving a bonbon dish. Afterward, they gave Mrs.Nellie Cockburn a shower.

Billy and Mary Roseanne visited with Grandma Wickwire and family Saturday evening. The precious grandson got his first inoculation and baby Nancy came back from the hospital. The children were greatly disappointed at Hallowe'en, as there was too much mud and rain to permit them to go out. If they couldn't get a treat, then a trick was probably out of the question.

Nov. 11th—Uncle Jack and Elly Joan visited Mildred and Rosebud and Mom Blenkinsop today. Mildred visited the home farm Tuesday and had dinner with Mom. Tulipbud blew out the candles on the cake. The precious grandson was also in the picture with his first tooth. All were sorry Rosebud was absent, not feeling too well.

Our good friend Frank Ghostkeeper had bad luck last week; one of his horses refused to go and laid down and died. Mr. Ghostkeeper was well on his way with the mail from Jackfish, and it made him later than usual.

Seen—Mr. Arnott getting his colts off behind the barn; and Mary Roseanne helping with the wood sawing while throwing the blocks to Dave Faibish; Uncle Jack having tea with the W.I. Ladies; Louis bringing Rosebud today to visit Grandma; Pop Blenkinsop taking his lambs to the Zaborskis.

Nov. 28th—The leaves are gone, the trees are bare, nature has a hazy look, seemingly waiting for winter, but the sunsets are as beautiful as ever. Oct. 21 was a grand evening always to be remembered at Spruce Glen, when Rev. and Mrs. Codwalloper and daughters Louella and Beth came from Jackfish Lake on their way to their new home in Medicine Hat, Alberta. The evening was spent with Mrs. Codwalloper playing the organ, all joining in songs. Aunt Elly Joan visited at Jackfish Lake this week. Mr. and Mrs. Wm. Blenkinsop went to Fort St. John today for medical treatment for their daughter. A rather lonesome pair came back, leaving Tulipbud in hospital for a few days.

Seen—Two policemen going north from Hines Creek on horseback. Rosebud running to meet her daddy.

Dec. 16—The Department of Public Works maintainer was over the roads this week and scraped the very icy roads. The W.I. held its monthly meeting at Aunt Elly Joan's this week. Quite a lot of business was discussed and a collection was taken for the Salvation Army appeal. A parcel to England was sent. Aunt Elly Joan served a delicious buffet lunch.

Seen—Lloyd Blenkinsop going for sawdust; Louis with a heavy load of freight. Smiling Chet Gilmour helping build onto the chicken coop. Chet says the reason hens have short legs is because if they were any taller, the eggs would smash with the fall.

Jan. 5—New Year's arrived quietly. A few people went to dances in Beaverlodge and Sexsmith; quiet family gatherings marked the day.

TO WHOEVER HAS MY WINCHESTER SHOTGUN

The hunting season is long past and I had to buy a new gun. You know where you can pump my old 12-gauge!

J.D. Levesque
Peace River

The Good Samaritan

Hal Sisson

An old-timer I once met said fifty percent of the time
we don't care about other people's problems; the rest
of the time, we're glad they're getting what they
deserve. I didn't buy this philosophy, so when a juvenile court judge asked for volunteers to straighten out
one misguided youth named Mitch Balfour, I agreed
to try to give him some guidance.

Mitch's parents were long gone and supervision by
his grandparents was minimal. A lot of do-gooders
had done their best for Mitch, mainly because they
recognized that the lad had talent and athletic ability,
especially at hockey.

There was a full-size pool table in my rec room,
along with a dart board and a well-stocked bar. I prid-
ed myself on being able to fix any cocktail a guest
might want. Mitch was a good stick at pool, as are most
hockey players. We played occasionally and Mitch

asked if he could come over and practice. I said sure. I had taken him under my wing and he was welcome.

Mitch would show up at my house at odd hours, usually around nine, play pool for half an hour then leave. I suggested he should practice more assiduously to become reasonably proficient at any sport, but still he only came every few days and stayed a short time at the table.

My wife soon began to suspect me of excessive drinking. At the same time, the RCMP uncovered a crash pad behind the walls of the activity room overlooking the ice at one end of the local hockey and skating arena, complete with mattress, booze and cigarettes. The pad belonged to Mitch, a good-looking kid who attracted a lot of girlfriends. The Mounties decided to charge him with bootlegging.

Every time he was at my house honing his snooker skills, Mitch had swiped a full bottle of spirits: scotch, rye, gin, rum or vodka, depending on the preference of the customer he had lined up for the sale. I shouldn't have exposed him to the temptation, so was I in the bootlegging business and didn't know it? As I was a defence lawyer who often gave the cops a bad time in court, I'm sure they at least considered the possibility, if they had thought they could prove collusion. But Mitch hadn't seen fit to take me in as a partner.

My losses were considerable, so I made a claim under my insurance policy. No insurance company to my knowledge has ever paid a claim before doing everything they or their lawyers can possibly think of to get out of it. All they want are the premiums. In this case, as invariably happens, my company refused to pay on the grounds that as each theft was individual, and as the value of each bottle was below the deductible, I had no valid claim. The company may have had a point, but they were as tricky as Mitch, and I felt I'd been had by both of them.

Mitch went on to play on the senior hockey team and showed so much talent that he was scouted by the NHL. When they asked him to attend a hockey camp, he refused on the grounds that they had already seen him play so they knew what he could do and he wasn't putting on a special show for their benefit. They might have given him a tryout even at that, if Mitch hadn't had such a chip on his shoulder and been such an anti-social renegade.

I got to the hockey rink midway through a game between the local Stampeders and the McLennan Redwings. My old client Johnny Delorme was standing behind the goal at the main entrance end of the arena. "Did you see it?" he asked.

"See what?"

"Did you see Mitch deck the referee? That'll show those bastards they can't get away with it all the time. They're always handing out those stupid penalties." I took it that Johnny didn't like penalties of any kind — figured the referees were unfair and only constituted unwarranted interference in the mayhem that usually goes on in any hockey game. Their only legitimate function in his eyes was to drop the puck at face-offs.

Mitch had received a two-minute penalty for high sticking, to which he took vehement exception. He got another two minutes for arguing and proceeded to the penalty box. Pondering the injustice of it all, and of the social system under which he lived, he decided on action. When the referee's back was turned at the next face-off, Mitch left the sin-bin, skated up from behind and blindsided the ref with a right hook to the head, breaking his jaw. They suspended him from the league for five years.

Mitch was embroiled in continual trouble with the law, but because of his youth, he generally got probation. The probation officer also did his best to help Mitch, for he had a likable side and the townspeople would really have preferred to see him succeed at something. When he decided to borrow the probation officer's car rather than steal it, he gained a three-day head start before his benefactor reported the matter. He was picked up several weeks later playing hockey in another province under an assumed name. But his chances for the big time were gone. No one could straighten Mitch out; he was his own worst enemy.

About a year later, early one summer Sunday morning when the sun was shining through the curtains on the bedroom door, something woke me up. I saw a shadow cross the light, and then someone began to stealthily climb the short outside staircase to the upper floor rec room—the one with the pool table. My immediate reaction was to jump out of bed, naked as a jaybird, jerk open the drapes and open the bedroom door. Two young boys immediately scattered in opposite directions; one over the garden fence toward the river, the other running around the house toward the front. I turned and ran through the house, grabbing my car keys on the way past the front door. The second would-be thief was through the driveway and into the residential street.

I jumped into my used Lincoln Continental to give chase and caught up to the boy about a block down the road. I pulled over to the curb and called to him through the open passenger side window. "What's your name?" I asked. He didn't reply, just picked up his pace. It was early in the morning and the street was deserted, but we were rapidly approaching the main drag.

I suddenly realized my situation. To any observer, including the cops, if they were to suddenly appear on the scene, a grown man, on a fine Sabbath morning, was cruising naked in a Lincoln, trying to pick up a male youth who was rapidly walking down the street minding his own business. Even I knew this was against the Lord's Day Act. Would the scarlet riders believe my story, or the one the kid might tell if he was as street-smart as Mitch—the guy from whom he had undoubtedly gotten the dope on the set-up and supply of booze in my games room. I have to admit I spoke harshly to the youth, told him to keep going and never darken my door again. Then I did a rapid U-turn in the street and went home.

For a long time afterward my wife referred to me as the Naked Narc.

Eulogy

Hal Sisson

I know for a fact that God has a sense of humour. If you don't believe me, just look around at each other. It's nice to be among friends—even though they're not mine—but just keep the following thought in mind. There's no such thing as a stranger; a stranger is only a friend you haven't met yet.

As you look about the audience today, just remember that many a ragged coat conceals an honest heart. More often a bottle of whiskey, but sometimes an honest heart. Remember, dear hearts and gentle people, that gratitude is riches and complaint is poverty and the worst I ever had was wonderful.

And now to the sad occasion that brings us all together here today. Dearly beloved, we are gathered here this morning in final solemn tribute to Dudley Fogducker, who is known to many of you as an honoured friend, a good father and a decent man. Personally, I wouldn't give you a plugged nickel for him. I never did trust him. In fact, I'm not sure he isn't up to something right now.

I know that look on his face. The SOB could be just faking, and I'm not just saying that because he was a lawyer. But having no talent wasn't enough to make Dudley a success in law, like it does for many many others. Dudley was so cheap and so perverted that he wrote out his last will and testament on his penis, but the probate judge said it wouldn't stand up in court.

I have to say this for Dudley, though: success— when he had any—success didn't change Dudley at all. He was still the same obnoxious slob he always was. Oops, did I say slob? Well, excuse me, that time I put in the *l*. The best thing Dudley had going for him was two chinchillas in heat.

I do know that his passing took something from some of us, because each time he passed, he took something from a few of us, until he cleaned out all of us. Although the worldly values of riches and gold are not true values, somebody out there is still going to have to come up with three thousand and eighty dollars to cover the flowers, the box the flowers came in, the funeral and the box that Dudley is in. He didn't even die a winner—we even had to buy a second-hand headstone. And under all those flowers, he isn't even wearing any pants! Let's face it, Dudley was cheap, and I mean CHEAP. And if his bereaved widow doesn't believe me, just let her go down to the Silver Spur Saloon and ask any of the girls down there.

That's not quite true—he never forgot the little people. He liked the little people. At the time of his death—at his age, death proved fatal—he was paying the rent for three midget go-go dancers. I've got underwear that's older than some of the girls he went out with.

When Dudley got married, he took his wife to Niagara Falls for their honeymoon. The Falls were her second biggest disappointment. She told Dudley he was a lousy lover. He said, "How can anyone make a value judgment like that in two minutes?"

His wife always wanted to have a girl, but they ended up having four boys. She called them Adolph, Rudolph, Get Off and Stay Off.

Dudley bought his wife a mink outfit—a rifle and a trap. No, he did buy his wife a coat, made of dog fur. Every time she passed a fire hydrant, her arm went up.

Dudley figured two could live as cheaply as one— a horse and a sparrow. Speaking of sparrows, when-ever I think of Dudley, I think of the Alberta Poultry Act—he was chickenshit. Dudley did a number on everybody: he called everybody number and every-body called him Number Two.

To those next of kin who may be truly grief-stricken in this hour of loss, I can only offer you the comfort of knowing that this is probably the best thing that could have happened to Dudley. For as the passing years fade, all who knew Dudley will remember him as the first to go to the sick, the needy and the unfortunate, with some word or deed to remind them that they were indeed sick, needy and unfortunate.

I think it therefore only a fitting gesture to close with one final word. He was a real...I'm sorry, I can't say that word out loud.

The Demented Concierge

Dwayne Rowe

Having reached the age of sixty recently and having sneaked a peek at actuarial tables, it's apparent that the Great Disposer, sometime within the next 12.3 years, is going to piss all over my chips.

The question then becomes wonderfully focused, not to the extent of knowing one faces the hangman in a fortnight, but more concentrated that the cerebral meanderings of relative youth. What does one want to do or be as the golden years approach?

For me, the answer is clear. I wish to spin out my declining years in a modest establishment featuring sleeping rooms, a large dining room and kitchen, salon, sun porch and yard. Not as a resident, but as a demented concierge.

I wish to be known as the kind of concierge who serves as the bogeyman for visiting grandchildren. The kind of person who one day will cheerfully comply with the suggestions of a tenant to replace a light bulb, and the next day refuse a reasonable request without explanation and stalk off glowering and muttering, then enter the garden for the sole purpose of kicking over some broccoli plants.

I'd like to be the kind of concierge who is approached only in the event of disaster, like falling-in roofs or crumbling walls, and then to be seen as an alternative more horrible than the unfolding catastrophe. The kind of concierge who isn't content with being snotty, arrogant, aloof, condescending, incompetent and a liar, but to go where no concierge has gone before—into the realm of the truly demented. The notice on the door of my room would be recycled from stolen hotel room signs that say *Ne pas déranger*, with *Do Not Disturb* on the reverse. I would clip off the *Ne pas* and leave *déranger*, which even the dumbest anglophone could decipher. The sign would be warning enough, like the ones that read *Rottweiler on the Premises*. Any potential whiner and sniveler needing concierge-type services would approach knowing up front the price to be paid.

As concierge déranger, I would replace lost keys with ones that weren't duplicates, merely keys found on the street. Some nights I'd jiggle with the heating controls so that the only two choices were heat or no heat, thus encouraging the two warring camps within the building to warm themselves on a bitter night by resorting to violence. Then, before dawn, I'd stalk the hallways, humming at a level just loud enough to penetrate the hearing of the occupants. Midday would find me boiling cabbage directly under the ventilation shafts, then stoking up on pork rinds, navy beans and positioning myself so that...

I would construct a little model garden and populate

it with slugs...hell, actually raise the slugs and give them away to tenants and visitors. As doorman in the evenings, I'd shine a flashlight into whitened faces and yell, "Passport!"

I'd order dairy products from the newspaper carrier, then curse at him for not having left the cottage cheese. I'd give out pass keys to itinerant missionaries and let them proceed directly, at any hour, to the rooms and proselytize their sleeping victims.

And when the end came, perhaps not naturally but at the hand of some jam tart who had somehow developed paranoid delusions during my term of office, it would be an inglorious and well-deserved exit. As for my surviving relatives, they could search for their roots and join genealogy groups or just sit around with friends and gossip about a weird ancestor, me, the man who used up his last slot of time as a demented concierge.

About the Authors

Hal Sisson was born in Moose Jaw, Saskatchewan. He was a reporter for the Saskatchewan *Star-Phoenix*, then a lawyer for thirty years in Alberta. He

Hal Sisson

retired in 1984 to devote time to croquet, marble collecting and writing. He and Dwayne Rowe founded the Peace Players, whose annual burlesque revue enjoyed a twenty-five-year run. Sisson's goal is "to write more fiction before bucket-kicking time." He lives in Victoria, BC.

Dwayne Rowe hails from northern Alberta, "so far up the map it made your nose bleed." He practised law with Hal Sisson in Peace River, Alberta from 1963 to 1969, and has defended clients or served as a judge in about a hundred and fifty Canadian communities, from St. John's to Old Crow. He has written comedy for CBC

Dwayne Rowe

radio and television and sold jokes to Joan RIvers. Rowe is a deputy judge of the Tax Court of Canada and lives in the seaside town of Sidney, BC.